KURT VONNEGUT
The Making of a Writer

DAN WAKEFIELD

TRIANGLE SQUARE

books for young readers

Seven Stories Press

NEW YORK ▪ OAKLAND ▪ LONDON

A TRIANGLE SQUARE BOOK FOR YOUNG READERS
PUBLISHED BY SEVEN STORIES PRESS

First trade paperback edition December 2024.

SEVEN STORIES PRESS
140 Watts Street
New York, NY 10013
www.sevenstories.com

College professors and high school and middle school teachers may order free examination
copies of Seven Stories Press titles. Visit https://www.sevenstories.com/pg/resources-
academics or email academics@sevenstories.com.

Library of Congress Cataloging-in-Publication Data

Names: Wakefield, Dan, author.
Title: Kurt Vonnegut : the making of a writer / by Dan Wakefield.
Description: New York : Seven Stories Press, [2022]
Identifiers: LCCN 2021061970 | ISBN 9781644211908 (hardcover) | ISBN
9781644214046 (paperback) | ISBN 9781644211915 (ebook)
Subjects: LCSH: Vonnegut, Kurt. | Authors, American--20th
century--Biography--Juvenile literature. | CYAC: Vonnegut, Kurt. |
Authors, American--20th century. | LCGFT: Biographies.
Classification: LCC PS3572.O5 Z935 2022 | DDC 813/.54
[B]--dc23/eng/20220526
LC record available at https://lccn.loc.gov/2021061970

Printed in the United States of America

2 4 6 8 9 7 5 3 1

KURT
VONNEGUT
The Making of a Writer

To Mark Vonnegut,
Karina Corrales,
Nathan Marquam,
and the memory of John Myers

CONTENTS

INTRODUCTION

When I was growing up in Indianapolis, the name Vonnegut referred to the hardware store. The headquarters of the Vonnegut Hardware Company was in a handsome six-story building downtown, while most neighborhoods in town, like my own small world of Broad Ripple, had its own branch. How else would your father get nails or your mother a can opener?

It was not until the spring semester of my senior year at Shortridge High School that I heard that one of our graduates, "the Vonnegut boy" (Kurt Vonnegut, Jr.), had published a story in *Collier's*, one of the leading weeklies in that golden age of magazines. (This was before most Americans had a TV, before the internet was even a dream of the future, and when reading stories was one of the three major forms of entertainment, along with watching movies and listening to the radio).

Those of us who wrote for the Shortridge *Daily Echo*, one of the only two daily high school papers in the US at the time, were inspired to learn that one of our own graduates, himself a former writer and editor for the *Echo*, had "made it" as a writer.

Even after I got to know Kurt Vonnegut as a writer and

a friend, it didn't dawn on me for a couple of years that he was from "the hardware store family." His only connection with the store had been brief: after his freshman year in high school, his uncle Franklin had given him a summer job working at the downtown hardware company headquarters. He had operated the freight elevator, running it up and down the six floors every day, and he had sometimes wrapped packages in the shipping department. Going up and down six floors every day was the opposite of inspirational, but Kurt felt a little sentimental about the business in later years. "I like what we sold," he once said. "It was all so honest and practical."

You could say the same for his stories, novels, and memoirs. And for the way he spoke. He said things that other people thought but didn't say or hadn't dared to think but recognized as true when they heard them. "The truth is often shocking," he wrote, "because we hear it so seldom."

He knew, before I did, that I would move back to our hometown of Indianapolis. I think that's why he told me one day in New York, seemingly out of the blue as we walked back to his house after lunch: "We never had to leave Indianapolis to be writers, because there are people there who are just as kind and just as mean, just as smart and just as dumb, as people anywhere else in the world."

I often have occasion to remember his words.

—Dan Wakefield

PART ONE

The Beginning

1.

THE BEGINNING

The house is big, and you are the smallest person in it. Closest is your artistic sister, who is five years older, and your scientific brother, who is three years more, and then your pipe-smoking architect father and your elegant society mother. They all have things to do and places to go—offices and lunches and parties and schools—which leaves you alone a lot except for Ida Young.

Ida is not a "nanny." She is the cook and housekeeper for your family, but she is much more than that. There is no adequate title for her. She is a black woman whom you know to be humane and wise, and she gives you decent moral instruction. She is exceedingly nice to you. She is as great an influence on you as anyone.

There is a saying that goes around during the Depression of the 1930s among black household workers: "Things got so bad, white folks had to raise their own children." Many well-to-do white families, like yours and the Blocks, who own the William H. Block Company department store

Bernard, Alice, and infant Kurt, the children
of Kurt Vonnegut, Sr. and Edith Leiber
Vonnegut, 1923-ish.

Kurt at about three.

in downtown Indianapolis, employ black women who are described in the census as "domestic workers."

White families who employ domestic workers often refer to them as "the help" or "our colored girl," but they aren't girls; they are women, and most of them do much more than cook the meals and clean the house.

Ida Young's grandson Owen says in an interview, "We were the recipients of the Vonneguts' 'hand-me-downs,' and it helped us survive because of the Depression. I remember it well."

Among themselves, the black women domestic workers refer to the "hand-me-downs" as "Thank-you-Ma'am bags." They are also given food to take home, leftovers from family meals. If a domestic worker has been with a family a long time, she may receive a remembrance in a will, any amount from $500 up to about $2,000.

After your family leaves the big brick house in the morning, it almost seems hollow, silent except for the barking of the bulldogs next door and the hum of traffic outside on Illinois Street and the clinking of dishes as Ida cleans up the kitchen after breakfast. She comes to you, wiping her hands on her apron, smiling.

Ida Young came to work for your family when she was thirty-nine. She has Thursdays and Sundays off. Her husband, Owen, works at the National Starch Factory, and together they own a house on Yandes Street. It's a twenty-eight-minute trolley ride from there to a stop a few blocks from your house that she can walk from.

The census takers say that Ida Young has "no schooling," but she teaches you to read. She knows the Bible by heart, and you know she finds wisdom and comfort there. She tells you stories of Jesus, like the one about the good Samaritan who helps the stranger whom others pass by. She tells you things that Jesus said, like when he went up on the mountain to give a sermon and told about the blessings people receive. You especially remember when Jesus said, "Blessed are the merciful, for they shall obtain mercy."

This one makes a deep impression on you.

Ida Young is a Christian, but she doesn't try to convert you to Christianity. Your family is from a long line of German "freethinkers," who believe in treating everyone with decency and respect but do not believe in God. In this country that outlook is carried on by the humanists and the Unitarian Church. Your family attends a Unitarian church on Christmas and Easter.

***

Your family takes you to a house on a bluff above a beautiful lake called Maxinkuckee where you're surrounded by other houses filled with other Vonneguts—aunts and uncles and cousins who all know who you are and call you K or Kay, which is what your family calls you because your name is Kurt, the same as your father's, and Kay seems nicer to them than Junior, which sometimes makes someone seem

smaller or lesser no matter how old they become. A home movie of your family in the magical setting of Maxinkuckee among all those Vonnegut relatives shows you smiling, so happy you do a little dance.

***

When you're five years old, your parents send you to leafy Orchard, a private school that your father helped found, set by trees in a beautiful field. There are just four boys and four girls to a class, and you make your first friend, Ben Hitz, and you meet a pretty little girl named Jane Cox.

***

Ida Young reads to you from a book she finds on your parents' bookshelves called *More Heart Throbs*. You think this book is very exciting stuff really, about bravery and heartbreak and all that. There are poems by great poets like Emily Dickinson and Christina Rossetti, as well as "Casey at the Bat," a baseball poem beloved by kids who like to recite it, and stories by Charles Dickens, Robert Louis Stevenson, and some anonymous writers for newspapers. Ida talks with you about the poems and stories she reads to you. She talks to you more than your mother does. She spends more time with you than your mother does.

***

Your mother is crying.

It's a chilly late afternoon in October when you're in the second grade at Orchard (about to be seven years old in November) and you've come home to see your mother with tears in her eyes. Your father is there too—he's come home early from work. You wonder what's wrong, and Allie takes you in the kitchen and explains that your parents lost everything. You look around and don't see anything missing. Ida Young is peeling potatoes she'll mash for dinner and serve with gravy along with chicken and lima beans and biscuits, and then chocolate pudding for dessert. You ask Allie where "everything" was lost.

"The market," she says and goes to her room, and you

know she doesn't mean the grocery store or the meat market but the "stock market."

Suddenly people are talking about it on the radio, and you see it in headlines in the *Star* and the *News*, the papers that come to your house every day. You hear about people in New York jumping out of windows of tall buildings because they lost all their money in the market, but you can't imagine your father with his pipe in his mouth or your mother in one of her party dresses jumping out of any windows.

You learn from Allie you won't have to go to the poor-house like people in the stories by Charles Dickens, but you will have to leave private Orchard and go to Public School #43, the James Whitcomb Riley School, named for the Hoosier poet. Allie gets to stay on and finish at Orchard, and your brother, Bernard, can finish at his private high school, Park, but there's not enough money for everyone to be in private school. You are only in the second grade, so maybe it's easiest for you to make the change. Anyway, that's what your parents have decided.

***

When your family gathers around a big table for breakfast and another big table in a bigger room for dinner, you're there but you're alone. You're left out. The talk flies thick and fast, but the only time the others stop and pay any attention to you is when you do something they think is funny, although you don't know it's funny until they look at you and smile and sometimes laugh, like when you spill a glass of water or when you think no one is looking and try to sneak an extra piece of something like the fried chicken Ida makes.

You figure out the way to get them to pay attention to you is to make them laugh, and it would be nice if you did it by saying something funny instead of doing something wrong or dumb. Radio comedians make you laugh, so you listen to them more closely and try to understand how they do it. You catch on that it's not just the words the comedians say that make people laugh but the way they say the words, and sometimes it's how they wait before saying a word that makes it funny. You listen to comedians Jack Benny and Fred Allen and Fibber McGee and Molly, who have the overstuffed closet that everything falls out of with a crash when they open the door, getting a big laugh. One holiday night around the dinner table your family is talking of New Year's Eve, and you speak up to ask a question: "You know where Father Time lives?"

"No. Where?" your brother asks, squinting skeptically.

"Times Square," you say.

That gets a few groans and giggles. Your sister, Alice, whom you call Allie, bops you on the arm and whispers, "You got that from Jack Benny!"

Another favorite of yours was the pair Vic and Sade, who

live "in the little white house halfway up in the next block" and sit on their front porch making goofy comments about the people who walk by. You read a story in the *Indianapolis Star* about a rich woman who died and left all her money to her cat.

"Remember that woman who left her money to her cat?" you ask at dinner one night. Everyone looks at you.

"What about her?" your father asks.

"The cat died and left the money to another cat."

That one does better than Father Time—you're learning how jokes are made.

You are also taken with comic book and serial characters who soar off into space and onto other planets like Buck Rogers riding in a rocket ship in the funny papers and the serials seen at the start of double features at the Vogue and Uptown theaters on Saturday afternoons. The future seems like a science fiction story.

***

You like the high-ceilinged hallways at School #43, and the teachers are kind and interested, and the kids are friendly. You like that one of the boys brings his dog to school every day and the teacher lets it sit beside him in class. You bring home friends from school whom your mother has never seen before, the sons of men who don't all work in offices. Some have jobs working on the line at Allison or Link-Belt or drive the streetcar or work at the Broad Ripple lumber-yard or sell insurance to people. The sons of these people have not been honored guests in your house before. When you go to their houses after school, their mothers give you homemade cookies, but they don't get cookies at your house, because your mother takes pride in not knowing how to cook. She was raised in a whole different world with different rules.

After you start at School #43, your mother takes you aside and assures you that when this Great Depression is over, you will swim with members of other leading families at the Indianapolis Athletic Club and play tennis and golf with them at the Woodstock Club. Does missing out on club activities make you sad? Not at all. She cannot under-stand that you'd rather hang out with the neighborhood kids—that to give up your friends at Public School #43 would for you be to give up everything.

Are you a sad child, knowing how rich your family was? Not at all. You are at least as well-off as most of the people you go to public school with, and you would lose all your friends if you started having servants again, and wearing expensive clothes again, and riding on ocean liners, and visiting German relatives in real castles.

Your house is for sale, but you don't have to leave it right away, because no one is buying big brick dream houses during the depths of the Depression. While your parents are waiting for someone to buy the place you grew up in, they sell some of their things, like expensive china and silverware, to people who come and take it right out of the house. Life goes on, but your mother doesn't get all dolled up and go to many fancy parties anymore. She spends her time writing stories she tries to sell to the big weekly magazines like *Collier's* and the *Saturday Evening Post* as a way of making money. Sometimes when your mother goes out at night now, it's not to dinners or parties but to classes to learn how to write. She doesn't have the knack, though. She doesn't know the taste of the audience, the ordinary people who read the popular magazines, so she never sells anything. But she keeps writing.

Your family no longer has a chauffeur or a yardman, but you still have Ida Young, who in a very deep way is your most important teacher, regardless of where you go to school. Ida doesn't talk to you only about Jesus and the Bible. She knows a lot about American history—things she and other black people have seen and marveled at and remember and still talk about, in Indiana and Illinois and Ohio and Kentucky.

One of the things that Ida Young and her family and friends talk about and never forget that happened in those states and others is the lynching of black people. Their own families, their brothers and sisters, mothers and fathers, grandmothers and grandfathers, aunts and uncles and cousins, were separated and sold and sometimes beaten, and after slavery was no longer legal, many of them were lynched—hung with nooses around their necks from trees. These lynchings were often occasions for white people to gather and gawk, and a photographer was usually there to take pictures of the lynching and sell them as souvenirs. It was common for some of the white people to send the photographs as postcards to their friends. Sometimes the bodies of the black people who were lynched were carved up and their body parts sold as souvenirs to white people.

Ida was born in 1883 in Kentucky, where there were lynchings of black people from 1880 to 1934 You are born in 1922, and a black person was lynched in Kentucky when you were five years old; when you were seven years old, two black boys were lynched in Marion, Indiana, just seventy miles north of where you live in Indianapolis.

The lynching that happens an hour and a half from where you live inspires a song called "Strange Fruit," referring to the bodies of people who had nooses of rope tied around their necks and were hung from trees and were seen in our American landscape for many years following the Civil War. The singer Billie Holiday sings that song like a dirge or a kind of hymn, something sacred. When she sings it at a club in Greenwich Village in New York City, the waiters stop and stand still, and everyone stops talking. You first hear the song on the radio when you are a junior in high school.

Hearing about history from Ida Young makes you more aware than most other white people of the denial of rights of black people in this country, the wrongs and damages done to them, the burning and killing of their sisters and brothers and mothers and fathers, the war that was fought to free them from being slaves, from being bought and sold like cattle by white people who owned them. Ida tells you history straight.

Ida Young is with you from the time of your birth to when you are ten years old and the big house you grew up in is finally sold. Your family moves to another nice but not so big house (but it's still pretty big as houses go, having four bedrooms) in the new town to the north called Williams Creek. Your family can't afford servants anymore, and your mother doesn't cook; she is still proud of not cooking. She was raised that way. Your father does the cooking now.

Ida Young's most important work is done. It wasn't the cooking and cleaning. She's prepared you; she was your prep school before you even went to school and after you started. She's prepared you to be who you are.

***

Lake Maxinkuckee is a place of magic in your life. You first went there as a small child with your sister, Allie, taking you around by the hand. You love being there. You love the water of the lake, so pure and cold, and all your life you prefer swimming in lakes to swimming in the ocean, which feels to you like "swimming in chicken soup."

It's not just the water itself that makes Lake Max-inkuckee so important to you. You make your first mental maps of the world on the shores of the lake when you are a child. Maxinkuckee is two and a half miles long and one and a half miles wide at its widest. Its shores are a closed loop. No matter where you find yourself on them, all you need to do to find your way home is to walk in one direction.

Isn't everyone's deepest understanding of time and space and, for that matter, destiny shaped by their earliest experiences with their geography, by the rules they learn about how to get home again? What is it that can make you feel, no matter how mistakenly, that you are on the right track, that you will soon be safe and sound at home again?

The closed loop of the lakeshore is certain to bring you home not only to your own family's unheated frame cottage on a bluff overlooking the lake but also to four adjacent cottages teeming with close relatives. The heads of those neighboring households, moreover, your father's generation, also spent their childhood summers at Maxinkuckee, meaning your family has been coming there almost since the lake's shores were inhabited by the Potawatomi Indians..

Every summer and into the fall throughout your childhood and adolescence, your family goes up there. Vonnegut relatives are all around in one of the real extended families you come to believe humans are designed to be part of.

By the time you are a man, the Vonneguts vanish from the lake just like the Potawatomi Indians, who were there before them. But it is always with you, imprinted in your mind.

You love to swim. You're not a natural at football and basketball and baseball, the sports that will make high school heroes, but Allie taught you to swim, and you're good at it. On a warm early November afternoon, you go to the lake with a goal in mind. You're eleven years old, and you are going to show your stuff by swimming clear across the lake at its widest point. Allie and Bernie get in the leaky rowboat, the *Beralikur*, which is named after all three of you. Your brother and sister lead you out into the lake as you swim behind the rowboat. You cross all one and a half miles of the width of the lake. You've done it. No matter what anyone says, you know you can do things with your body as well as your mind. This day means a lot. The lake means a lot. It always will. It is imprinted in your mind.

2.

POPULAR/UNPOPULAR

You walk into Shortridge, and you know your life is changed. Not just because it's a high school—it's not just *any* high school. It's the only high school in the country with its own daily paper, the Shortridge *Daily Echo*. It's the only high school in your city of Indianapolis or state of Indiana that sends some of its grads every year to colleges in the East—Harvard, Columbia, Dartmouth, Yale, Vassar, Smith, Radcliffe.

As you approach the front doors of Shortridge facing Meridian Street, the three-story brick building that takes up a city block looks impressive, and its high-ceilinged halls seem to echo with the school's history. Above the stage of Caleb Mills Hall, the school's grand auditorium, are the words of its namesake that students commit to memory: "A disciplined mind and a cultivated heart are elements of power."

You have a chemistry teacher who's a real chemist, Frank Wade. Your brother comes over to listen to Frank Wade from his hotshot private Park School. You have an English teacher named Marguerite Young who's written a novel,

Shortridge High School, Meridian and Thirty-fourth streets.

and now she's writing a biography of Eugene V. Debs, a workingman from Terre Haute, Indiana, who ran for president on the Socialist ticket five times and got millions of votes. Your teacher of ancient history is Minnie Lloyd, whom you think should be wearing medals for all she did at the Battle of Thermopylae.

Besides the great teachers, there is an energy from the students, in the hallways. You can feel it in the sense of purpose, the way the lockers bang quickly open and shut between classes, the intense pitch of talk and laughter in the halls, the way the girls wear their white socks pulled up high from their saddle shoes (not like the girls at Broad Ripple, who wear their socks rolled down to their ankles).

At the sectionals of the state basketball tournament, the student fans from all the city schools are jammed into Butler Fieldhouse. When the Shortridge team comes out on the floor, the students from all the other city schools boo because they're jealous. They have this cheer just for you, for your own proud high school: "Shortridge, Shortridge, Shortridge is *it*—*s-h* for Shortridge, *i-t* for *it*!"

Yeah, they are right—you are *it*!

It can be overwhelming, too much all at once, but you have your best buddies there with you—Ben Hitz and Vic Jose, Skip Failey and Bud Gillespie, neighbors and friends, some from as far back as kindergarten. You meet before class in the mornings in the cafeteria so you know you're not alone in this powerhouse place.

You see right away that the cool kids belong to clubs—not the school clubs like the Fiction Club and the Drama Club, but social clubs like D.A.W.G. and C.R.A.G. for the jocks and Euvola and Sub Deb for the girls. Sometimes the names behind the initials are secret and sacred and sometimes not—your friend Majie Failey tells you the initials for her club, P.D., stand for "Pixilated Debutants." There are almost as many clubs as there are students.

You hear that joining a club is "a rite of passage." But you have to be asked to join. How long does it take to get to know people and have them know you well enough for them to know they want you to be in their club? You and your friends realize it may take forever and may never happen—none of you are jocks who go out for football or basketball. So instead of waiting around to see if you make an impression on people in the clubs, you form your own club. Now you and your buddies don't need to hold your breath and worry and hope to be picked by a club, that near-mystical rite of passage. You guys make your own rite of passage. You are the O.W.L.S. You wear little silver pins that look like owls. (O.W.L.S. doesn't refer to wisdom, as in a "wise old owl"; it's based on a club you read about in the funny papers—you got it from Major Hoople, a funny fat guy in a comic strip who belongs to the Owls Club). You and your buddies learn how to belong.

Though not connected to school, another teenage rite of passage for many children from families who want them to have the best advantages is taking Mrs. Gates' Dancing Class, held at the very proper Propylaeum building downtown. For the most part, the girls like getting dressed up for these occasions and boys hate it—among the indignities for male teens is not only having to put on a suit or sport coat with a tie for each dreaded lesson but also being required to wear white gloves. They *itch*. Mrs. Gates is imperious, a straight-backed woman with hair coiled atop her head.

She reminds you of a duchess, and you aren't about to get on her bad side. When your buddy Skip Failey spreads BB shot over the dance floor, you keep dancing, managing to keep from slipping and sliding, and guide your partner as others give up and go to the sidelines, laughing.

You get good grades in the courses you like—English and history and public speaking—and do well enough to pass in math and the sciences. Your uncle Franklin gives you a summer job after freshman year, operating the freight elevator at the six-story downtown headquarters of the Vonnegut Hardware Company.

Back at school for sophomore year, you start to shine—you get elected to the student council. You are piling up the honors, the achievements that will bloom below your picture in the *Annual* when you graduate. You joke that the list of achievements below your senior picture in the yearbook is your "first obituary."

Vonnegut, Kurt Snarfield
Student Council, '38, '40. President, Social Committee. Drama League. Press Club. Co-editor, Tuesday's Echo, '40. Liner staff of the Annual. "B" band. R.O.T.C. Junior pin and ring committee.Entertainment committee, Junior party. Co-chairman, winning act, Junior Vaudeville, '39. Vaudeville, '40. Round-up, '38, '39. President, O.W.L.S. Club. Chemistry. Cornell University.

Girls notice you and like you, which makes the jocks not like you at all. In spite of your swimming across Lake Maxinkuckee when you were eleven years old, you are not a high school athlete. You're a tall, thin, gangly kid with a mop of blond hair and long arms and legs that seem to flail about heedlessly. You are not designed for sports like football and basketball. Maybe you're the antijock—a smart guy with a sense of humor who isn't one of the high school guys you call "the sports gods."

Your name is linked with a girl in one of the popular gossip columns in the *Echo* when you're a freshman. The jocks don't like that. They are supposed to be "the ladies' men." One of the football players sees you walking with a pretty girl between classes, and he bumps into you, knocking your books all over the hall. These torments follow you like demons through high school. Your friend Majie Failey says the jocks bully you, make fun of you.

In English class you read a parable by Benjamin Franklin about his buying a whistle when he was a little boy, whistling all over the house to everyone's annoyance, neglecting other things to spend his time whistling, and finding out he paid too much for the whistle—it was not worth it after all. Franklin uses this example to warn people about spending too much time and money on things that don't matter at the expense of things that are more important to them.

Your class is given an assignment to write about a current example of spending too much money and time on "whistle purchasing." Instead of writing a philosophical response, you come up with an entertaining story. Your teacher thinks it's worthy of publication in the Shortridge *Daily Echo*. The editors agree, and your story appears as "This Business of Whistle Purchasing (Apologies to Benjamin Franklin)."

* * *

During my primary education, my sense of competition overcame my better judgment.

She had taken the school by storm with an irresistible southern accent. At that time the supreme social achievement was a date with said sophisticate. At last proper connections were made and the time set for Sunday afternoon. I had visualized in my innocent little mind a simple jaunt to perhaps a neighborhood house then as a finale the local Sweet Shoppe. I arrived a bit early and patiently waited. After a period she shouted out to me that I might be calling a cab. Just a bit taken aback, I decided this perhaps was the thing to do, and followed her instructions. She was ready when the cab arrived and asked me which downtown picture house I had in mind. Now utterly disarmed and disillusioned I blurted out one theater far above my means. The die having been cast I proceeded to my financial doom! With the expenditure of eighty cents we were admitted to see a show which afterwards she blandly stated 'wasn't worth a plugged nickel.' I heartily agreed.

On the way to the bus we encountered a confectioner's. The windows were adorned with dozens of tiny shamrocks. Fearlessly I looked in—after all they were only ten cents. To my dismay I found her to be admiring the fifty-cent centerpiece. Somehow I bought her this thing with the saleswoman telling me how lucky I was, as it was the last one, believe it or not. I got her home on the bus after one twenty-five cent banana split. Her last words at home were 'Thank you so much. Ah had a gawges time.'

Did I pay too much for my whistle? I should say not!

Your name follows. It is the first of many times it will appear in the *Echo* before you graduate.

Your "Whistle Purchasing" story is light and funny, but maybe the most telling thing about it is that it is a *story* by standard definitions of a story: it has a beginning, a middle, and an end. You didn't learn to write one in a class; you just knew how. Ida Young read you stories; you heard Jack Benny and Fred Allen tell stories. The form is in you.

You start writing regular columns for the *Echo* called Inquiring Reporter and Bull Session. You introduce a subject people are talking about, like the new "swing" music that's becoming popular, and then you get students' opinions: "Many Sunday afternoons about our house have been marred by heated debates over swing and classical music. Many's the time I've seen great salt tears of indignation form in the eyes upon hearing some classic tortured by new tempos. What does the youth of today think? Is it the racy thing of gaudy tastes and disregard for the musical treasures of the past? This subject has been discussed by Inquiring Reporters since time immemorial."

You then act as "Inquiring Reporter" and ask other students their opinions: "Patty the Cassler said, 'Sometimes I think it's sort of a dirty shame to dope up Wagner with drums and vibraharp. But you've got to admit that 'Reverie' and 'Your Love' (jazzed up Tchaikovsky) are a wee bit on the O.K. side.' We don't gotta admit it, but we will."

In one of your Bull Session columns on "The Care and Feeding of Problem Parents," you write:

> When a child turns out to be unbearably nasty he is shipped away to some institution specializing in the subduing of brats or perhaps given some pills to better his or her disposition. What about the adult offender? For centuries, the youth of the world has been confronted with the sometimes unbearable actions of their emotionally unstable parents and few words have been spoken in regards to this age old tyranny! Listed below are a few case histories given to me in strictest confidence by numerous worried offspring.
>
> A common complaint, brought to me by many sons and daughters of prominent Indianapolis families, is that their parents often wait up for them to come home from dates. The only result of this unreasonable action is that the entire family harmony is shattered for sometimes so long as a week. The person who foolishly waited up (usually the mother)

Popular/Unpopular

27

probably goes about the house grumbling over the sleep lost in the incident while the righteously indignant child wonders why it should make any difference to anyone what time he or she gets in as long as he or she does get in. Not one parent in ten can give a logical answer to this question!

The right people seem to appear in your life at the right time. Sometimes students take the *Echo* home after school, and sometimes parents read the paper. One of the mothers who reads the *Echo* is Phoebe Hurty, an advertising copywriter for the William H. Block Company, one of the big downtown department stores. She likes what you write and sees that you write often; she hires you to write advertising copy for the *Echo* about the clothes that Block's Department Store sells to teenagers. The deal is that you wear the clothes that you write about to school, and you pose as a model in ads that the store makes for its teenage clothes.

Phoebe Hurty becomes your mentor. Her legal name is Gladys Sutton Craig Hurty, but she doesn't see herself as a Gladys, so she picked out a name she thinks suits her better: Phoebe. She uses another name for the advice column she writes for the *Indianapolis Times*: Jane Jordan. Her advice is to the point and practical.

A girl writes to tell "Jane Jordan" that she likes a boy who was respectful and nice, but on her last date with him, he'd been drinking and said if she really cared about him, she'd "surrender." Here is "Jane Jordan's" advice: "I think I would ignore the incident. If he behaves properly when he is sober, enjoy his company, and avoid him when he drinks."

In an interview in the *Indianapolis Times*, Phoebe tells about her philosophy for raising her two sons to become independent.

"When they were very little, the garage was their playhouse," she says, and one cold day they started a fire to keep warm. Phoebe came home from work to find the street clogged with fire trucks. The fire the boys had made to keep warm had nearly burned down the garage. Phoebe says her son Bobby "gave me one agonized look and said, 'Mother, I will eat turnips.' I saw that he wanted to be punished to relieve his sense of guilt and that in his opinion, nothing could be worse than turnips. So we had turnips for dinner and nothing more was said. We've never had a fire since."

You get to be friends with Phoebe and her sons Robert, who is a year older than you, and David, who is a year younger, and you hang out at their house all the time.

Phoebe Hurty talks bawdily to you and her sons and to your girlfriends when you bring them around. She's funny. She's liberating. She teaches you and her sons to be impolite in conversation, not only about sexual matters, but also about American history and famous heroes, about the distribution of wealth, about everything.

Phoebe Hurty makes such an impression on you that thirty-five years later you dedicate your novel *Breakfast of Champions* to her. You write, "I keep trying to imitate the

Popular/Unpopular

29

impoliteness which was so graceful in Phoebe Hurty." All those years later, you still remember an ad she wrote for an end-of-the-summer sale on straw hats: "For prices like this, you can run them through your horse and put them on your roses."

You want your column for Block's clothes to be a little impolite, like the kind of copy Phoebe writes, so you call it Block's Sniffer. The name comes from the time you were writing something in room 240, the office of the *Echo*, and you absent-mindedly sniffed your armpits. Several people saw you do it, and after that you were given the nickname Snarf. You write about everything Block's is selling for teenagers, from the long key chains that boys are sporting to Palm Beach suits for graduation to the latest in saddle shoes:

> If the cookie of the hour winces while looking you in the face, or has ever expressed dissatisfaction at some of its features, attract her attention to your feet! BLOCK'S has stocked its first floor shoe store with the most complete line of springtime tugboat accessories in town. Drape your eyeballs over the following illustration [of shoes], and see if these gadgets aren't a wee bit on the O.K. side, Wedge soles are the thing, lad. . . . They come in soft white or tan leather for six bucks, or in brown reversed calf $7.50. Ask for "Coolies"—this is just a trade name for foot heaven.

Of course, the jocks who don't like you are even more annoyed when they see you in Block's ads for clothes with good-looking girls.

* * *

Not only are you writing a lot (it's fun and easy for you), but you're also reading a lot, and not just assignments for class. You read *Prejudices* by H. L. Mencken, the newspaperman and critic who makes fun of middle-class moralists (he calls them "the booboisee"), Mark Twain's *Huckleberry Finn* and *Tom Sawyer*, and short stories by Hemingway and Saki and O. Henry. Your talks with your father seem strained and "distant," but his younger brother, Alex, who graduated from Harvard, talks easily with you and gives you books like Thorstein Veblen's *Theory of the Leisure Class*, which makes fun of the social pretensions and possessions important to your parents, especially your mother. She was raised to be that way. Her father was a wealthy brewer, and he sent her to Europe, where she visited castles and had her "coming out" to society party in London, where German officers in shiny black boots clicked their heels and bowed to her.

* * *

Your father is not flooded with architectural assignments in 1937, but one of the smallest commissions he gets turns out to be one of the most important for *you*. Hillis Howie, a teacher who has now become principal of Orchard School, has been leading groups of boys on a "Western Trek" to a camp he established in New Mexico in 1925. The summer

Popular/Unpopular

after your freshman year, Mr. Howie asks your father to design six houses that will become a permanent part of the Trek headquarters on land Howie bought near Gallup, New Mexico, a 480-acre area known as Cottonwood Gulch. When Howie asks your father what his fee will be for the designs, he says, "Tuition for my son for the Western Trek."

Howie takes you and your friend Ben Hitz and fourteen other boys on a trek in three station wagons to the "Wild West," through Colorado, Utah, New Mexico, and Arizona, sleeping outdoors every night and burying your own dung. One night Mr. Howie scares you and the other boys half to death on purpose, screaming like a wildcat near your camp, and a real wildcat screams back!

You learn the names of plants and animals and what they need to do to stay alive. You all have specific missions from the Field Museum in Chicago. You are a "mammalogist," and you put "traplines" out every night. You actually catch a subspecies of the tawny white-footed mouse that has not been seen before.

Mr. Howie introduces you to Ben Henio, a Navajo man whom he met and befriended on his second trip to Cottonwood Gulch in New Mexico in 1926. Through Mr. Henio and other Navajos, you learn firsthand about the Navajo culture. This trip awakens you, expands your understanding and imagination to your natural surroundings.

***

The biggest thing at Shortridge High School besides the *Echo* (aside from football and basketball, of course) is the Junior Vaudeville, an annual show of musical and dramatic acts written, directed, and acted by students of the junior class. This is such a big deal that Hollywood talent scouts actually come to see the show (one of the Vaudeville acts a few years after you graduate is written up in *Life* magazine, and the boy who wrote, directed, and starred in the act is invited to spend a summer working at a Hollywood studio). You and your friend Ben Hitz write, direct, produce, and perform in a Vaudeville act called "Dangerous Dan McGrew," inspired by the Robert W. Service poem "The Shooting of Dan McGrew," which some guys recite around campfires or during intermissions at dances to get some laughs and entertain their dates ("A bunch of the boys were whooping it up in the Malamute Saloon. . . ."). Your act wins the prize for the best act of the Vaudeville.

You're elected president of the Social Committee, which plans the dances. You play clarinet in the school band, belong to the Fiction Club with a girl named Madelyn Pugh who will become an inspiration as a writer of *I Love Lucy*, the premier popular TV sitcom.

* * *

After your junior year, you recruit two friends to join you on a great adventure, a new western trek, not the "official one" led by Orchard principal Hillis Howie, but an independent one, just you and your friends taking the same route across the Rockies and down into New Mexico to the original Trek camp of Mr. Howie.

Your friend George Jeffrey's father will supply you with camping equipment (a tent and a one-burner stove). Bud Gillespie's father loans you a car, a Packard with a rumble seat (a pulldown seat at the back of a car where the trunk is today, which could also be used for storage). Your father supplies you with two shotguns from his gun collection for protection from wild beasts or highway robbers. Just as importantly he gives you a letter affirming that the three of you are good boys, are responsible with firearms, and will not cause any trouble. For good measure, he also gives you a letter on the stationery of the Children's Museum (he was one of the founders) stating that you are on a mission for the museum.

You plan to keep a diary, a record that you think of as a book about your travels. You give it a title, *The Rover Boys in the Southwest*, borrowing the name of a popular series of adventure books for boys that was published from 1899 to 1926 and remained in print for many years afterward. The Rover Boys, like The Hardy Boys and the Nancy Drew mysteries, are bywords of entertainment for young people in this period before the dawn of television. They are part of the innocent culture of adolescence in America before World War II.

You don't take the Rover Boys books seriously—you are reading the plays of George Bernard Shaw and social criticism of newspaper columnist H. L. Mencken and sociologist Thorstein Veblen. You use *The Rover Boys* as a kind of spoofing title of what was in fact a real adventure of three high school boys making the type of trip the Rover Boys books depicted, on their own in 1939 for two months. Almost as important, your families supply you with a treasure trove of canned sardines.

Here are a few samples of your daily entries from the trip. You vow to write every day on this trip—many people say they will write every day for a certain period of time, but few really do it. The fact that you do write every day of this trip means that you are a real writer. Probably giving the book a name—as if it's a whole story—helps you to stick to that. You are not just writing a diary; you are writing *The Rover Boys*.

MONDAY JULY 31ST:

Dear Family:

Left Home Sweet Home and those we hold dear to us at 5:40 on the nose. Apparently only I was able to convince my parents that bed was the logical place for their kind. As we pulled away, none of us quite realized the magnitude of the thing we were about to undertake. We all cheered lustily as we turned from Meridian to West Washington Street, and

the wind-shield compass proudly displayed its big white "W."
Bud was at the wheel and at every corner of his hometown,
asked "Which way?" I have a feeling that his total lack of a
sense of direction or any geographical memory will be the
basis of many interesting adventures for the month to come.

At the first filling station George relieved his phenomenal
bladder, which will slow us down considerably—this proves
to be interesting!

Rolling western Indiana gave way to honest-to-God
Illinois plains, which seem to be extremely functional, but
exceptionally boring. Bud had on his high-heeled boots and
was already looking for a fellow cowhand. We rotated every
100 miles and kept at a constant 50 m.p.h.

At noon, we crossed the "Father of the Waters," and held
up traffic in order that Bud and George might fully realize
the solemnity and symbolism of their first crossing. At Han-
nibal, Mo, Bud insisted on seeing a tourist fake called, "Mark
Twain's Cave." After a furious struggle, we dragged him away
from the miserable pot-hole and moved on—he insists on
seeing every foul thing advertised along the highway.

The spot we chose to eat lunch upon was occupied also
by a long discarded corn crib, which Bud obstinately insisted
was inhabited by Missouri share-croppers. We approached
with exaggerated caution and met resistance offered by only a
belligerent bee which stung poor George upon the wrist! He
bewailed his plight the entire afternoon and demanded why
he should always be the object of the wrath of the Gods. He

was constantly showing us how it had swollen and claimed that it had in some way affected his injured toe. We ate the food that we had so condescendingly accepted from our parents and threw kisses to the East.

Golly, it's easy to get sick of the plains—corn, wheat, soybeans, and horizon. Why can't they grow zinnias or something interesting and friendly? George suggested orchids!

WEDNESDAY 2ND:

We all arose early with Bud singing deep tones from his unlimited repertoire. It suddenly dawned upon us that we were not alone. Sitting calmly upon his horse was a tall, loose-jointed, cowhand. He must have sat there in silent mirth over our antics for at least ten minutes. We expected to be thrown bodily from the premises, but our laconic friend merely grinned. He disappeared as unexpectedly as he had come.

At about 11:00 we caught our first glimpses of the Rockies—(Pike's Peak Group). We put in an extra quart of oil, filled up the tank and started up Pike's Peak at noon. The Packard boiled constantly, and we had much trouble reaching the summit. (Bud is constantly clamoring for a 10-gallon hat and blames George and me for his failure to get one). At the top, Bud wrote postcards to his friends, while George and I climbed about the Peak for choice photos. While up there, the two of us met a darned cute girl from Kansas. We utterly defamed Bud in our conversation to protect our new find from his well-known charms. Her name is Betty Schwitzer, but I doubt if we'll ever see her again. Such is the unhappy lot of the transient.

I drove on the way down through hail and sleet, and the unguarded hairpin turns extracted groans from my two passengers which made me feel they had as little faith in my driving as myself. . . .

. . . Between Manitou and Denver . . . a fiery argument over whether we should see Buffalo Bill's grave or not left us all mute and sullen. Bud is pro—George and I are con. Bud is convinced he is being persecuted.

We hit Denver at about 6:00 and bought some groceries. Among our purchases was a bag of sugar which soon permeated every nook and crevice of both ourselves and the car. We asked a wise little guy how we could get to road 87. Said he, with a twinkle in his eye, "Did you say 87 or 87?" This was the first opportunity to use our rifle, but George kept a cool head and stayed my murderous hand.

For dinner we broke out a can of corned beef and cabbage which was perfect. Our camp was just outside of Denver, and we could watch the city light up as night fell. A beautiful "blood moon" rose before us and caused us all to be quiet and pensive. We found we had parked in a necker's haven and were surrounded by silent couples. Bud and I decided to stalk one car and took the ever-handy corn knife as protection. We terminated the plan, however, as we figured we had a fair chance of being shot, especially if approaching with such a terrifying weapon. The wind toyed with the tent all night but turbulent flappings failed to mar our rest.

SATURDAY 5TH:

. . . Instead of beans for breakfast we feasted upon cocoa, eggs, and wholewheat bread. I'm getting sick of this part of the Rockies and would like to move on. Bud keeps blaming me for little things like no gun toting cowboys. His spirits were buoyed, however, when he found out that Grand Lake was the highest registered yacht anchorage in the *world*! As George was still away, Bud and I rented a canoe after whittling the proprietor to half the regular price. Neither one of us had ever spent much time in this type of boat, and so provided those on shore with an hour of solid comedy.

George pulled into camp just in time to drink some ox-tail soup I was preparing. George likes to be by himself as he is sulking over something. I believe it's because he insisted the potatoes were not a starch, but green things"—while Bud and I told him he was wrong. George hates to be told he is wrong about something so we do it as little as possible.

MONDAY 7TH:

We slithered out of dank bedding and consumed a clammy breakfast. We moved like automatons in dismantling the humid camp—three minds with but a single thought—let's get the hell out of here!

The watch has ceased to function so we have no idea what time it is. Several major operations have been performed with knives, forks, and hammers, but it still remains aloof to the time of day.

The road leading down from the mesa was a gelatinous mass of clay. We had little control over the car and depended on the slimy ruts to guide the wheels. The car is in perfect harmony with the West, as it now has a two-inch protective finish of adobe and other local types of clay.

The radio is on the blink, except for certain isolated periods when the car is stopped—it then concedes to wail dubiously for a couple of minutes before failing totally. Sometimes we can restore it by opening the car door or pushing in the cigarette lighter. Phenomenal country—the West.

Once off the mesa we stopped for breakfast at Cedaredge. A very swell fellow and his wife operated a clean little lunchroom. They gave us all the pancakes we could eat for 25¢. This offer, I believe, he regretted making—but kept on smiling and being friendly as we complacently munched away his profits. Every meal we buy out here costs us 2¢ in taxes.

FRIDAY IITH:

For once I beat George at getting up early. I assembled my rifle and went in search of any form of meat. No bird or beast for bones. On one side of the road I found the complete bone structure of a cow and vertebrae from a sheep. I intend to use those sheep vertebrae as a very rugged tie rack for my room.

Jeff and I got breakfast as usual while Bud lay in bed and grinned his big friendly smile. He just sits or lies around at meal-time and sings "Ragtime Cowboy" until his meal is ready. He gets very angry if told he doesn't do his share—as there isn't terribly much to do, George and I preserve the peace by saying nothing. George will never forgive me for having taught Bud "Ragtime Cowboy," and I have often considered self-extinction. It was quite early so we killed time by writing until time for the stores to open.

You and your buddies drive to the headquarters of Hillis Howie's annual Western Trek in New Mexico, the trip you took with Ben Hitz two years ago. Now you introduce Bud and George to Mr. Howie and his camp at Cottonwood Gulch.

THURSDAY 17TH:

. . . Mr. Howie generously assured us that we were welcome to stay for as long as we wished. Jeff quickly made friends with the cook, and we dined on the leftovers from the Trek breakfast.

Our consciences drove us to the point where we were willing to earn our keep. We toted water and adobe clay for a new roof for the flashy stone latrine. Mr. Howie failed to notice our efforts, and later in the afternoon, asked us if we would like to earn our keep. Wearily, we filled up the holes and ruts with boulders and clay to check erosion. That evening, we were allowed to eat with the others... no scraps ... all first-hand grub.

There was big talk going around about the final campfire of the year for the boys on this year's Trek. Satires were being prepared on phases of camp life and we were quite left in the cold.

After the light part of the campfire program, the entire group did a beautiful job of singing a number of Indian songs. Each trekker placed a stone around the fire in the final ceremony. I am ashamed to say that I had quite forgotten what the one I had placed there two years ago looked like.

We made plans to depart before the Trek in the morning, and dropped off to sleep in a bedroom decorated beautifully by mama nature.

Bud Gillespie's father has arranged with his friend Frank Phillips of Phillips Petroleum for you, Bud, and George to stay at his Woolaroc Ranch outside of Bartlesville, Oklahoma.

SATURDAY 26TH:

... At Oklahoma City, we drove to the center of town in search of a gentleman Mr. Gillespie wished us to look up. We parked in a "no parking area" for about an hour while Bud went to his office and called his home. The man was on a vacation so we went out to Spencer to locate some land the Gillespies own with a test oil well on it. We found the well miles back in thick, backwoods country. The test was down 6400 feet, and due to go 400 more. A roughneck talked to Jeff and me on the technique of the business and was quite instructive. To drill a test well costs $100,000, and only one in 67 tests gives oil. We also found out that this wasn't Gillespie property, but decided to let it go at that.

From Spencer we got on the wrong road and had to take an intricate series of trails and by-ways to again be on our correct course. While on one of these, night fell and we made camp in a pasture. While we were brewing supper, the owner came over and talked for hours on end. He seemed to have traveled all over the nation, yet he could never remember the name of towns or people. His conversation was full of "Whatchamacallits" and "Oh, you know where I means." We gently hinted at his departure by crawling into our sleeping bags and pulling blankets over our heads, which had an effect in due time.

At midnight, the heavens drizzled upon our un-tented selves. I covered my bed with the poncho. Jeff remained secure in his waterproof bag, and Bud slept sound and serene. The minor deluge ceased at such stoicism and the remainder of the night was dry.

At 3:00 I was awakened by a queer instinctive feeling of not being alone. The camp was surrounded by cattle! One cow (with a crumpled horn) was complacently chewing my poncho. Others were examining the faces and general appearances of the still sleeping Jeffrey and Gillespie. George awakened upon contact of a wet bovine proboscis. He bounded out of bed like a madman and hit the nearest beef full on the pate with a milk bottle. With a unanimous bellow, the entire group broke into a stampede to thunder away deep into the night.

Your time at Woolaroc Ranch turns out to be a great finale to your trip. The Phillips family is on vacation in Europe, but they have instructed the ranch hands and staff to take the best care of you and your friends. You eat fabulous meals cooked by a chef and served by waiters; you are given good cigars to smoke and shown to a rec room that features a player piano. You ride horses as ranch hands take you through cattle and buffalo herds and explore the three-hundred-plus acres of the ranch. After four days it's time to head home.

THURSDAY 31ST:

The less said about this day the better. . . . We got into the car at six o'clock in the morning. We drove like hell with the damned E on the compass staring us in the face all the way. The seven hundred miles between Bartlesville and home melted completely by midnight, and we each sneaked into our bedroom without awakening a soul.

. . . Darned if I didn't weep my fool head off. . . . And that same night I almost laughed that same head off thinking of all the uproariously funny things that happened. The only

way I'll ever really be happy will be out there under the stars.
. . . Damn but that's wonderful!

***

For the second time, you are elected president of the Social Committee, this time for your senior year. Despite your determination to see yourself as "unpopular," the number of times your name comes up in the *Echo* this year makes you seem like the highest-flying social butterfly. You begin by planning the first dance, which you name the Gym Jam Jump, and the season is underway.

You report in your Bull Session column of October 3, 1939, that Howe High School has hired the imperious Mrs. Gates to teach a course in "hoofing, plain and fancy." Not to be outdone, "Shortridge has procured the services of ex-grad Eleanor Hopwood to give instruction in the corner of the gym to those with uneducated feet." In one of your ads for Block's Department Store, you note, "The ever present saddle shoe still ranks as topflight footwear. Spike heels irking nearly everyone. Gals who wear socks with high heels are unanimously felt to be lousily dressed."

Models and entertainers for Block's Department Store ads are listed as:

Shortridge: Kurt Vonnegut
Tudor Hall: Jane Cox

You write an Advice to the Lovelorn column:

Why don't I rate any of Barbara Kiger's affections?
—K. Vonnegut

Dear Kurt,
You're up against Gene Williams' monopoly.

***

You write, "BLOCK'S PREP HOP is the only place to go.
In case you haven't heard, an authority informed me that
Midnight Blue is the accepted hue for this year's tux."
  Your sign-off for the column Block's Sniffer is sometimes
"KOORT II" and other times "Kurt Snarfield Vonnegut II."
In a column advertising aftershave lotion, you write:

I was once waiting about thinking of weighty things when
I heard a couple of babes blowing off about how neat it was
when their dates radiated a gentle aroma of aftershave lotion.
  One gal, a wonderful little blonde, raved so much about it
that I sped home and drenched myself in six different kinds
of the stuff. I was forced to take it all off, however—I was
unable to leave the house without being followed by crowds
of women, all inhaling deeply!

A gossip column notes in May: "Marge Geupel has marked Don King off her list. Some say, too bad, but Kurt Vonnegut has a place on her list in June."

The Bluebelle and Uglyman dance determines the ten most popular girls and the ten most popular boys in the senior class, and you are one of the ten chosen as candidates for "Uglyman." There is no higher social rank at Shortridge High School.

Most of the "Uglymen" are either football or basketball stars. The jocks who don't like you are really driven up the wall by your crashing the popularity ranks. One of them grabs you after school in an otherwise empty hallway and crams you into one of the big school trash cans.

It's humiliating, but that's not all. There's a dance after school where several teachers give "joke presents" to some of the seniors, and the football coach, in front of everyone, gives you a subscription to the "Charles Atlas Bodybuilding Course." Charles Atlas is a famous body builder, and high school kids laugh at his ads, which show a comic strip of a skinny kid at the beach with his girlfriend. A big bully— maybe like the jocks who make fun of you—kicks sand in the face of the boy to embarrass him in front of his girlfriend. The ad and the "Charles Atlas Bodybuilding Course" do not seem funny to you, because you see your-self as "a skinny, narrow-shouldered boy." There are a lot of laughs, and you leave feeling humiliated.

Maybe those are the days you look back on some sixty

Candidates for Uglyman.

years later when you write in the introduction to *Bagombo Snuff Box*, a book of your stories, "Imagine that it is 1938 again. . . . I come home from yet another lousy day at Shortridge High School. . . . It is raining outside, and I am unpopular."

Can this be the same Kurt Vonnegut who's one of the ten most popular boys in the senior class, who's an editor of the Tuesday edition of the *Echo*, who writes columns for the paper, and who put on the winning Junior Vaudeville act?

You sign your senior picture in the yearbook, the permanent record of your high school years, "Kurt Snarfield Vonnegut."

3.

CORNELL

High school seemed like forever, but now it's over! The next step for many of your friends is college. Ben Hitz is going to Harvard. Vic Jose is going to Swarthmore, and so is Jane Cox, the girl whom you knew in kindergarten at the Orchard School. Swarthmore is a liberal arts college, and your father wouldn't go for that. The lack of architecture jobs during the Depression has disillusioned him with his own profession. He got very few commissions from 1929 to 1940.

"Be anything but an architect," he tells you, and your brother, Bernie, dismisses the arts in general; he says they're not serious, just "decoration." Your father wants you to be a chemist like your brother. He doesn't want you to waste your time and his money on subjects he considers "ornamental," like much junk jewelry—literature, history, philosophy.

Even though you have to study scientific subjects, you want to keep writing, which feels natural to you. You loved writing for the *Echo*, and H. L. Mencken makes newspaper reporting seem adventurous and fun in books like *Newspaper Days*. Mencken carries on Phoebe Hurty's lessons on how to be impolite in writing. You know that Ernest Hemingway, the big-time writer from neighboring Illinois, got his start as a reporter for the *Kansas City Star*. You're surprised to learn you could get a job right now as a reporter for the *Indianapolis Times*, the paper where Phoebe writes her entertainingly impolite advertising copy. That won't fly with your father, though; he and Bernie think you ought to go to college to study something "serious," which to them means science.

"Chemistry was everything then," you later recall. "It was a magic word."

Bernie majored in chemistry at MIT, and your father and Bernie want you to study chemistry, physics, and math. You don't think you've done well on the college board exam in chemistry, so MIT—where your father and Bernie went to college—is not in the cards. A great-uncle and a cousin went to Cornell, and Bernie and your father think that's a good choice.

Though your science-minded family doesn't realize it, they are sending you to one of the best possible colleges for someone who wants to write, to serve an apprenticeship on a newspaper. Just as Shortridge has the first daily high school newspaper in the country, Cornell has the oldest independent daily college newspaper in the country; you are drawn to it like a magnet when you first step on to the campus. The *Cornell Daily Sun* is in fact a real newspaper (it is a corporation entirely separate from the university), coming out every day but Sunday, featuring national as well as campus news on its front page and available on newsstands in Ithaca, New York, Cornell's hometown. You easily pass a journalistic tryout for the paper and start writing for it. The paper's office is your haven, your new home base.

You join Delta Upsilon, your father's fraternity. He comes to the fraternity house when you're going through hell week. Is he trying to make sure you're safe, or does he want to see if you can take it? You survive. The fraternity has a lot of engineering students, but you find your college family at the *Sun*. Miller Harris, who's a year older than you, becomes editor in chief of the *Sun* as well as your mentor and friend.

You don't like your freshman English teacher, and the feeling is mutual. You don't care, because you're going to be a chemist (although you are flunking calculus). It's a requirement that you pass freshman English, which you think is a pain in the neck, and you convey that to the teacher. You think he's a jerk, and things get so bad that he threatens to throw you out of the course. He gives you a make-or-break assignment, one last chance to redeem yourself—write an essay on Henry David Thoreau.

It so happens that you already know quite a bit about Thoreau, who is one of your favorites. At Shortridge High

School, you read classics like *Moby-Dick*, Mark Twain's *Life on The Mississippi*, and Thoreau's *Walden*, his account of going to live alone in a cabin in the woods by Walden Pond. He wanted to live simply, and you especially like his advice "Beware of all enterprises that require new clothes." Since you already know all about Thoreau, you don't have to do any research. Having written for the *Daily Echo* three or four times a week throughout most of high school, you've become a fast typist, so you knock out this essay with speed and ease. With an air of casual triumph, you deliver the paper to the teacher the next day. You stride out of the building with your head held high, and walking down the flight of stairs outside the building, you fall and break your ankle. When the teacher calls you in to talk about your essay, you are on crutches.

The teacher is impressed with your writing, and he wonders why your other papers haven't been up to par. You say that since you're going to be a scientist, writing is a tiresome chore for you (though not when you're writing for the *Sun*.)

Your happiest times at Cornell are when you're all alone (like Thoreau!) and it's very late at night, and you're walking up the hill after having helped put the *Sun* to bed. Even though you're an agnostic, when you trudge up that hill, you know that God approves of you.

A world-traveling visitor to the campus tells you that Cornell is the forty-ninth greatest university in the world.

You had hoped it would be in the high teens! Little do you know that going to an "only marginally great university" will help make you a writer.

"That is how you get to be a writer," you say later, "incidentally: you feel somehow marginal, somehow slightly off-balance all the time."

You were bullied by jocks at Shortridge, but now at Cornell, you try to outthink them—think ahead of them. There is an all-fraternity run that you are supposed to take part in. You know that your long arms and legs flail around rather than enabling you to be adept at the major sports, football, basketball, and baseball—you're not even a fast runner. To avoid people joking about you as a slowpoke, you show up at the big fraternity running event in pajamas that are too small for you and a cap with a tassel. You make it a joke, and you don't have to run, avoiding humiliation.

You make sure, as you always do, to find ways to relieve the boredom of some of your courses. That spring you are put on academic probation. You are kicked out of ROTC for writing a column called "We Impress *Life* Magazine with Our Role in National Defense," in which you tell how you and your fellow future officers fooled a *Life* photographer while pretending to carry on efficient drills that you and the others invented on the spot, barking orders with technical-sounding nonsense words.

***

The summer before your sophomore year, you take some courses at Butler University in your hometown, thinking good grades in English courses might be able to be transferred and help your academic standing at Cornell. You also take a science course, but your heart isn't really in any of it. You decide that Butler is a place for turning out insurance agents—anyway, that's your excuse for dropping out.

After plenty of high school girlfriends and a swoony summer romance at Lake Maxinkuckee with a beauty from ritzy Grosse Pointe, Michigan, you've forgotten about Jane Cox when you go to a party at Woodstock, Indianapolis's hotshot country club, and run into her—the girl you knew back at the Orchard School from kindergarten to third grade. Now she's a very pretty young woman and smart too. You and Jane connect, talking a mile a minute, and you want her to come and see you at Cornell when she goes to Swarthmore. So that the conversation will continue, you give Jane a copy of Emerson's essays.

Back at Cornell, you announce in a column in the *Sun*, "You haven't met Jane yet—she'll be up here for the Fall House Party—we're getting married in '45, you know."

You don't play it cool about your feelings for Jane. The prospect of seeing her makes you feel like a romance novel writer. You are tempted to write purple passages about bodies melting into each other. You think up all the lovey-dovey names you have ever heard and want to string them together to capture her. You are really going all out, pouring out your hopes and dreams. In the terms of the times, you are "going all the way" to tell her how important she is to your feverish creative process. You know she will inspire you to write better books if she will agree to be your muse. There is no stopping you as long as you have her beautiful face in your mind's eye. You would rather think of Jane than any of the cardboard silhouettes of pinup girls that decorate the walls of soldiers' barracks.

As an underclassman, you are not allowed to practice the high art of column-writing, which supposedly can only be done by time-tested veterans. But of course, they are not counting on the kind of inspiration that she provides you with, which enables you to do far more than the untested aspiring Grantland Rices. Of course, there is a formula for writing on the sports page. You can't get away with writing in plain English. You have to learn the tricks of the trade. You hope, after learning those tricks, that you can forget them. You don't like the boring assignments doled out to sophomores. In your first column for the *Sun*, "Innocents Abroad," you simply pass on jokes.

Soon, though, you start addressing the big issue of the era: America's involvement in World War II. You think America ought to stay out of it. You come from a long line of pacifists, and in grade school you were proud that America is not "warlike"—that the US has a small standing army and generals don't predominate in Washington. In your column in the *Sun*, you defend the rights of students to remain in school. You defend Charles Lindbergh, who became a hero when he made the first transatlantic flight and is now leading the cause of "isolationism."

One Sunday in December of your sophomore year, you are hanging out at your frat house when news comes that mobilizes you into journalistic action. The Japanese have bombed the American naval fleet at Pearl Harbor, Hawaii. You rush to the *Sun* office and help put out an edition of the paper that hits the street with a headline you wrote above stories from the Associated Press: "JAPS START WAR ON U.S."

After Pearl Harbor, Germany and Italy join Japan in declaring war on the US, but you still defend Lindbergh and the isolationists, who don't want us to open a "second front" in Europe to help England hold off Hitler's Nazi war machine. Your newspaper notes under one of your columns that they are not the opinions of the *Sun*.

On September 29 of 1942, you continue your stand against the US fighting in Europe. You write in your Well All Right column a sharp takedown of your fellow Hoosier Wendell Willkie. The former Republican candidate for president has gone to London in hopes of persuading America to come to the rescue of England in its battle against Nazi Germany. You describe Willkie as a "political yo-yo from the Hoosier State [who] has demanded a second front—while wearing a rumpled blue serge suit with egg on the vest. This homespun corporation lawyer, probably the last presidential candidate to be born anywhere near a log cabin, has set all England . . . yapping like a pack of underfed dogs in a kennel."

To not so subtly undercut Mr. Willkie's ideas, you point out that "Wendell Willkie went to Indiana University, not West Point; he studied law, not military science."

On November 13, 1942, you write:

> We the student body of Cornell University do perfectly understand our relation to the war effort. Either we work or enter immediately into the armed forces. Our work here has a value to the nation—otherwise, the war department never would have sanctioned educational war deferments and reserve programs. Each student has his own conscience in the delicate problem of "here on borrowed time." It is not necessary that the university furnish one for him.
>
> There are those here to change completely our ways, often needlessly. Persons with cracker barrel patriotism [are] molding [our] now-pliable Cornell into new and grotesque patterns.

Your writing for the *Sun* is not limited to matters of war and politics. You find an even juicer subject in going to an all-night gambling club.

"Well All Right" by Kurt Vonnegut: In Which We Dare To
Enter The Stronghold of Evil

One of a group of party boys at Zinck's suggested that
we go over to XYZ Club. Playing along like we knew what
the XYZ Club was, we followed the gang.

Down South Aurora Street, over the small concrete
bridge, and through an unmarked side door, the six of us
found ourselves in a small, windowless, heatless, rugless
hallway, facing another door. A bored pair of watery eyes
peered at us through a small panel in the second door,
looked us over as a matter of form, then let us in. The door-
keeper shuffled down another fire-trap corridor into the
main room.

It was surprisingly large, and appeared more so because
of the absence of furniture. Green lamp shades partly
covered naked light bulbs, suspended from smoky heights
by long knotted wires. Men in shiny blue serge and shirt-
sleeves ran dice and card games and sold chips over felt
green table-tops. The only fixture on the expanse of cheap
wooden wall was a certificate which declared under grimy
glass that the place was legally recognized by the State of
New York as the Ithaca Social Club.

All the Cornellians we saw were at the dice table. We
watched a fraternity brother lose twelve dollars which a
veteran kibitzer said was peanuts compared to what some
fellows lose in an evening.

Somehow, our first trip to a gambling hall didn't pack the kick we thought it would. We left it with its bad air, its opaque window shades, and its neat stack of chips.

***

You are still corresponding with Jane, but she has made clear that she is free to date whomever else she wants to see. She is not going to give up being the "belle of the ball." From what you hear, one of her suitors has taken the lead—and it's not you. Rumor through the grapevine has let you know that a fellow named Bates may have forged ahead to the front of her love-line. You write to Jane and pose what seems to you an essential question in this dilemma: what is she going to do with you if she decides to marry Bates?

You are put on academic probation again in the spring of your sophomore year, and when you return to Cornell as a junior in the fall, you don't do much better in your science classes. In December, you come down with pneumonia and are flunking chemistry. You go home at Christmas and decide not to return to Cornell.

Instead of waiting to be drafted, you decide to enlist in the army in January of the New Year. This is not just "a way out" of your problems; you have decided this is a war that is worth fighting and that must be fought. By this time there are few who still oppose joining the fight against Hitler's Germany. We are fighting Japan in the Pacific and

Germany and Italy in Europe and in Africa. The country is united as never before. Local "air raid wardens" make sure lights are out in cities that practice "blackouts," families on "the home front" raise "victory gardens" in backyards, Boy Scouts collect scrap metal for the war effort, and flags appear in windows of houses with blue stars for sons in service and gold stars for those who have died in action.

You flunk your physical exam for the army in January—the doctor says you still have pneumonia and you're underweight. You try again in March, and this time they take you. You're sent to Fort Bragg, North Carolina. Imagining you might become Indiana's answer to Tolstoy, the great Russian author of *War and Peace*, you take your typewriter with you. Maybe you want to announce your intentions—establish your identity as a writer—so you leave your typewriter on top of your bed. Some other soldier—maybe a budding Hemingway—takes it.

4.

WAR

The army prepares you for war by sending you back to school! Maybe they will send you to journalism school so you can write for the army newspaper, *Yank*. You apply to be a clerk-typist, which might lead to some kind of writing job. No such luck. You are in the Army Specialized Training Program (ASTP), a program intended to turn out officers with college degrees. You are going to Carnegie Mellon University and the University of Tennessee. Your assignment is to study mechanical engineering; as you hit the books, you are also learning how to work with other soldiers to load and fire the largest mobile weapon in the US Army—the 240-millimeter howitzer. This monster comes in six pieces; before it can be fired, you and your crew have to put it together. It seems as if you have to invent it every time you fire it. It seems to you like "the ultimate terror weapon—of the Franco-Prussian war."

* * *

You still have room in your head to think about Jane.

From what you hear from her, it seems that you'll both be coming home around the same time. You get the idea from reading her letters that she's not the same girl you knew when she left. You've been telling her that you love her for several years, and the information doesn't seem to have any effect. There is one thing you know for sure about what you call "our relationship"— she seems to be the only person you really like to write to. You don't know why that is. You don't know if it means "I love you." Surely it must mean, at the very least, that she's your best friend.

Before you get your engineering degree or have to help load that howitzer, the Army Specialized Training Program is canceled in the spring of 1944. Infantry troops are needed now for the war in Europe. The army sends you to train as an intelligence and reconnaissance scout at Camp Atterbury, outside Indianapolis. You learn how to read maps and aerial photos and engage in hand-to-hand combat.

Your army training gives you something that proves to be essential to you during war (and after)—a friend. At Camp Atterbury, your sergeant says to choose a buddy. Maybe with Mutt and Jeff, the tall and short comic-strip characters, in mind, you team up with Bernard V. O'Hare, a Pennsylvania Irish Catholic who smokes as much as you do and has a sense of humor that matches yours. The sergeant tells you and O'Hare that now you are buddies. You are to share everything during the war—blankets, food, water, ammunition.

The best part of training at Atterbury is that you're only forty miles from home. You'll get to visit your family. Your mother and father still live in the smaller but comfortable house that your father designed in the new development of Williams Creek, a pleasant woodsy area north of town. The house has four bedrooms, a library, and a two-car garage, but your mother regards living there as a comedown from the city's high society. Your father does the cooking, since your mother was brought up to feel that cooking is beneath her—cooking is for servants like Ida Young, but your family can't afford to bring Ida Young or anyone else back and forth from the city to Williams Creek. Your mother's efforts to make money by selling short stories to the well-paying weekly magazines has come to nothing. She writes about the glamorous days of her upper-class youth, with castles and duchesses and fancy balls and private boxes at the opera, but the popular magazines want stories about the lives of the kind of middle-class Americans who read them. Your mother grieves that she has fallen below her formerly high-class station in life.

You get a three-day pass on Mother's Day weekend and come home wearing your uniform with everything shined to impress the folks. You're happy that your sister, Allie, is there while her husband, James Adams, is away in the service. Allie wakes you on Sunday morning and asks you to go with her to see what's wrong with your mother. You and Allie find your mother curled up as if sleeping. You realize that she is not going to wake. She has died from an overdose of sleeping pills. Thankfully, she looks peaceful. You feel a rush of emotion, of all the love you held back when you were growing up. You realize now her complete devotion to her family. You realize now her dedication to the life of each one of you. You can feel her pride in what you accomplished. You wonder why we don't have the power to express these things before it is too late.

In the weeks following your mother's death, Jane writes you a warm and understanding letter. You realize how important her friendship has always been in your life.

* * *

On June 6, General Dwight D. Eisenhower leads American and British troops in the invasion of Nazi-held Europe, the historic "D-day." This opening of "the second front" in the war against Japan and Germany, the long-awaited commitment that you opposed while writing for the *Cornell Daily Sun*, is now something you celebrate. You join the parade around the Circle, the heart of downtown Indianapolis on June 15 in a celebration of D-day. The US is now fighting Japan in the South Pacific and Germany in Europe.

* * *

Jane is graduating from Swarthmore as a model student with all honors. She did it the right way, without making false turns or falling into educational potholes. You, on the other hand, did a kind of patchwork job, collecting what information you could and trying to hold it together so that it amounted to something. You are very happy that you get to see Jane again in fifteen days, when you'll be at Atterbury and Jane will be home visiting her mother. Hopefully can present yourself as a worthy candidate for her love. The odds against you seem great. She is seeing other men, many of them probably far more accomplished than you. You have to go into battle with what you have and the strength of your love.

You make an all-out pitch for her to finally marry you. She turns down your dramatic proposal, and she leaves for Washington, DC, to work as a clerk-analyst for the Office of Strategic Services (OSS), the predecessor of the CIA. You and your division spend September packing to go overseas. It's a huge job to pack all of the equipment needed to fight the war. In the midst of your preparations for war, you have a pressing concern about Jane: whether or not she is pregnant with your child. You hold your breath for several weeks until you get the signal that Jane was not pregnant.

***

You leave for England on October 17 on the *Queen Elizabeth*, once a glamorous ocean liner that carried tourists and business travelers to and from Europe; now it is painted gray and lined with bunks for American soldiers on their way to the war. When you arrive in Cheltenham, England two weeks later, before being sent off to what will inevitably be some kind of battle scene in Belgium, you write one last time asking Jane to marry you. Now, you can go to war with your mind clear, knowing that you have made every effort for the thing you most desire: a life with Jane.

You and your division cross the English Channel on December 6 and go ashore at Le Havre in France. You are part of the 106th Division, which is hurled into the last great battle of the war in Europe, the Battle of the Bulge. In one last major effort to turn the tide that is rolling against it, Hitler's army throws all it has against the weakest part of the line of Allied troops. None of the men in your entire division have been in combat before, most of them unmarried young men, many, like you, pulled from the engineering programs of the ASTP and hurriedly given training in hand-to-hand combat. Your division replaces a weary division at the front, not knowing that the Germans have slipped behind your lines, cutting you off from the main army. Your regimental commander is promised parachute drops of supplies and ammunition, but the awful wintry weather grounds the flights. A Nazi general calls this last-ditch effort "Autumn Fog," after the fog that provides cover for the massing of two hundred thousand German troops and six hundred tanks of the powerful panzer divisions.

On December 16, outside of a small town in Belgium, the shooting war begins for you. Shells from railroad guns rain down as you run for cover, and hundreds are killed in the heavy bombardment. Your regimental commander calls for supplies and ammunition, but radios are blocked and the skies, thick with fog, prevent airdrops.

On the nineteenth, you and your buddy Bernard O'Hare are part of a six-man reconnaissance team ordered by your regimental commander to go out into the fog—a fog that may hide the enemy behind every tree, around every hill— and try to find your own artillery. In other words, Private Vonnegut, you and your whole regiment are lost.

You and the other reconnaissance scouts crawl through the snow, across the frozen ground. It's less than a week before Christmas. The snow-covered landscape could be a Christmas scene, except the trees are bare, and instead of bells there are distant pings of bullets and the muffled boom of heavy guns. Your mind flashes to snowy hills of childhood in Indianapolis, the cold air stinging your cheeks, the rush of speed thrilling as you go on your sled, belly down, face forward, into the kissing wind. Now you go slow, on your belly on the frozen ground, all your senses alert. Do or die. Lie low. All you see is snow.

The Germans wear white; you wear green. Olive drab— it doesn't matter. You stick out like a sore thumb. You find some fellow soldiers in a bit of a hollow and join them for warmth and seeming safety, at least a respite, but the brief rest is shattered by a loudspeaker booming an order in a German accent: "We can see you. Give up!"

You and your fellow soldiers fix bayonets, but iron and explosions fill the air above you, felling and wounding some, killing one soldier near you. The loudspeaker commands: "Come out!"

You disassemble your rifle as you've been taught, and you and your comrades throw down your guns and throw up your hands in surrender, asking your white-clad captors not to shoot.

You put your hands over your head as you come out, and the Germans look at your dog tags. "Vonnegut" is not a common German name, but being paired with "Kurt" (pronounced "Koort") makes it very German. One of your captors asks why you are making war on your German brothers. You explain that you feel no more connection with Germans than with Brazilians. You took two years of German in high school, but your parents didn't talk much about their German heritage, speak German often at home, or teach it to you and your sister and brother.

During World War I, when America sent "our boys" overseas to fight the Germans on the side of the British and the French, a wave of anti-German sentiment swept the country, including your hometown of Indianapolis. Americans sang the patriotic song "Over There": "Over there, over there . . . the Yanks are coming, the Yanks are coming. . . . Send the word, send the word to beware." The Germans were the ones who had to beware, not only their army in Europe, but also German Americans born in the United States who were suspected of being spies or "collaborators" or at least sympathizers with the enemy of the moment. The beautiful building in downtown Indianapolis designed by your architect grandfather, a hub of cultural and gymnastic events and training known as Das Deutsch House, was splashed with yellow paint. Its name was changed to the Athenaeum. Your father received an anonymous letter telling him, "You better not teach your kids Dutch."

You are marched with thousands of other American prisoners for several days until you come to a railroad siding. There are lines of boxcars that brought in the German troops, and now you and the other Americans are shoved into them like cattle—but not with as much room as cattle would be given. The Germans herd you into cars and stuff the cars as full of bodies as possible. There is no room to sit down, much less lie down, and air comes in only from vents; there are no toilets. This is no fraternity "hell week." This is hell, the real thing, for two days. They let you out at night to sleep on the ground in the snow, and some die of frostbite. The next day, others die when some of the boxcars are hit by British bombers who think the trains carry supplies for the Germans. According to international agreements, railroad cars with the wounded are supposed to be marked with red crosses, and cars with prisoners are supposed to be marked with orange and black stripes so they won't be bombed, but evidently there isn't any orange or black paint available. One car with only officers in it is destroyed.

They are picking men at random who will go farther on to work as laborers in the city of Dresden, which is supposed to be an "open city," not to be bombed, as it has no war factories or concentrations of troops stationed there. It is a city known internationally for its art and museums and architecture. Many people are sentimental about Dresden.

When you get there and the big doors of the boxcars slide open, you see the first beautiful European city you have ever seen. It is gorgeous. You have seen New York and Boston, and you have seen the buildings in Indianapolis designed by your grandfather and your father, but now you understand why nations agree that this is an "open city," a treasure not to be destroyed by bombs. Dresden is a world city like Paris, so the people of the city don't expect to be hit.

In Dresden you are assigned to live in an underground slaughterhouse, "Slaughterhouse Five," and you share it with 150 other prisoners, 12 guards, and the carcasses of countless cattle and pigs.

You are one of a half-dozen prisoners who are able to speak some German, and you are interviewed to be the translator who will convey the Germans' orders to the other prisoners and the prisoners' complaints and requests to the guards. Your two years of high school German get you the position. Your first job is to go with other prisoners to clean up rubble from a minor bombing attack, a mistake. At the end of the day's work, you and the other prisoners are given watery soup and a piece of black bread each. In the morning, you get another piece of black bread with watery coffee.

You go to work every day at different factories. Your big break comes when you're assigned to work in a factory making malt syrup. The syrup is given to pregnant German women who need vitamins and minerals that are lacking in their wartime diet. You and the other prisoners who work in the malt factory make excuses to go through the room where the malt is being packed so you can sneak spoonfuls of it for yourselves. You remember the cod liver oil you were given every night when you were growing up in Indianapolis, which was thought to be a cure-all to make children healthy. It tasted awful. The malt syrup probably helps you, but the spoonfuls you sneak of it aren't enough to stop the pellagra you get that polka-dots your legs with ulcers, nor is it enough to stop the hunger.

A fellow prisoner from the hard streets of New York has sucked up to the Nazi sergeant, telling him all men should be brothers, war is hell, and the Germans are good people, after all. You call him a collaborator, and he tells you to "brighten up." He has a black market going on, and he can get you as much as two loaves of bread for your wristwatch. Two loaves of bread sounds like a banquet, and you make the deal. When Louis comes to your bunk that night, he says he could get you only one loaf of bread—the market is glutted with watches. When you seem upset with the deal, he offers to take back the bread and return your watch, but you can't give up the feast of a whole loaf.

Later there are crumbs spilling down from the bunk of the prisoner above you—he is chewing his way through two loaves of bread that he got for his watch along with ten cigarettes! Back home in Indiana, you thought that being an Eagle Scout was the way to prepare for successfully making your way through life, but now you wonder if Hell's Kitchen is a better preparation than the Beaver patrol.

As if things aren't hard enough, a teenage Nazi comes swaggering in from the nearby countryside to join the guards. His uncle is mayor of an outlying town, which qualifies him to have his own rifle and strut around. He delights in calling the prisoners "Chicago gangsters" and making their lives miserable. One day, a prisoner who is ill but has been made to work is leaning over a table he is cleaning, and the teenager, who has been nicknamed "Junior" by the prisoners, prods the sick man with his rifle to make him work harder.

When the prisoner can't do any better, Junior hits him in the ribs with his rifle. You yell at Junior, "You fucking swine!" Junior knocks you out with his rifle, and the next day, you are put on trial by the guards. They accuse you of insulting the fatherland. Your rights as translator and representative of the prisoners are taken away. The guards give you a beating, leaving a cut that will remain as a scar behind your left ear. After that, you continue to be taunted by Junior, who tries to make you crack, but you keep your temper. You think of those high school jocks who bullied you; at least they didn't have rifles.

On the night of February 13, 1945, air raid sirens go off just before ten o'clock at night. The city is having its annual celebration of Shrove Tuesday, and the celebrants are coming home from parties. They hurry for shelter as you and the prisoners go down to your quarters in the underground slaughterhouse. You figure it must be another false alarm, that the target is a city not far from you, maybe Leipzig.

What you start to hear tells you the target is not another city. It is Dresden. It is you. Thank God you are deep underground. Even there it is scary as hell. First you hear the booms, distant and coming closer. Then they are on top of you—like giants walking on the ground above you. Bombs become booms become booms. They keep coming. You look at the floor. You clasp your hands on your head. You try to shut out what is happening. Someone speaks.

"I wonder what the poor people are doing tonight?"

The tension cracks. A couple of laughs come. It makes no sense. Nothing makes sense. You're glad you're down deep in the earth in your slaughterhouse. The real slaughterhouse is above.

In the morning you all come out and look around. The sky is blue. The city is gone. You take a deep breath. The air is hot. You take a step. The ground is hot. Rocks look radiant, almost glowing.

The guards don't know what to do with you. There's no one they can ask. Someone directs them to a camp out of town that turns out to be a prisoners' camp of South Africans from the British army. The guards move you in with them. They wonder what to do next. There's no one to report to; there are no communications.

Either the guards find some officers, or some officers find them. They block off the city to German citizens. It's not safe. Only the POWs are allowed to go into it. You and the other prisoners are ordered to go in and dig out the dead bodies. Your job is to shovel the corpses out of the shells of broken buildings, out of cellars, and put them in piles that become funeral pyres. After a while, the job of shoveling thousands of corpses becomes too much, so flamethrowers are used to destroy the corpses. There is looting of the broken buildings by guards and prisoners. For prisoners, looting is an offense punishable by death. One half-starving soldier takes a can of green beans from the wreckage of a house and tries to hide it under his coat. A guard sees the lump in his coat and discovers the can of beans. You watch the execution, and the next morning, you are part of the group ordered to dig the graves of the man who stole the beans and four other prisoners accused of looting. You and the other prisoners assigned to this detail cover the graves.

You and your fellow prisoners are always hungry. You think about food all the time. You talk about your favorite food with your buddies. Your favorite food, your favorite meal. A few of you find notebooks and pencils in some of the buildings and hide them. You write down your favorite meals and the food you love. You write down what you and your buddies dream about: stacks of pancakes with eggs in between and covered with honey, hot fudge sundaes with cherries and whipped cream and nuts. You describe one another's Thanksgiving dinners. Some imagine cheeseburgers with everything; one imagines steak with mashed potatoes and butter and gravy. You think of candy bars— Snickers, 3 Musketeers, Mars bars, Hershey's.

Someone in the town with a radio says the American troops are only a day away. You and the other prisoners are marched out of the city, and the Germans leave you and disappear into the woods. The Russians get there first, and the scene is chaotic. You and five of your buddies, including O'Hare, find a horse and wagon, paint a star indicating the US on the side of the wagon, and take off toward France. You're just a few hours away from France when the Russians take you prisoners to exchange you for Russian prisoners held by Americans. You and the other prisoners of war are sent to a Red Cross Center in France.

You must feel an extraordinary sense of power as you sit at a table, a free man, with pencil and paper. You also feel a responsibility to tell your family in a few words what you had just experienced. As you start to write, it seems as if the hardships, the hunger, the pain, of the last months acted almost as editors of your prose. There is nothing fancy in what you write. You stick close to the bone. The scenes you describe of shoveling bodies in piles to be extinguished by flamethrowers after the devastating bombing of the city of Dresden are vivid for their plainness, their understatement of raw brutality. You intersperse like a refrain the irony that among all this death, you survive. This letter becomes, in a sense, the announcement of yourself as a writer.

***

You arrive home from the war on the Fourth of July. Germany surrendered several months before, and US troops are closing in on Japan. Your family comes to get you at Camp Atterbury outside Indianapolis. Your father, your uncle Alex, and your sister, Allie, are in the party there to retrieve you. Uncle Alex spots a tall, very thin soldier in the distance and wonders if it can be you. It is, but it's a you that's forty-three pounds lighter. You want to drive the car home, and you talk a mile a minute. You're through with the war, the army, and what you call the whole bloody mess.

5.

MARRIAGE AND CHICAGO

You get back to the States at Newport News, Virginia, in June, but there is more paperwork, a tangle of red tape. It seems to take forever before you are finally granted your well-deserved sixty-day leave, which gets you back to Indianapolis, to your family and Jane. She has graduated with honors from Swarthmore and will be home from her job in Washington, DC, to visit her mother. Your first order of business is to make a new all-out effort to get her to marry you. Your friend Victor Jose, who also went to Swarthmore, warns you that Jane is considering another man's offer. It is not Bates. It's a successor to Bates. Another man from Swarthmore. There's no time to waste.

When you go to pick up Jane at her parents' house, you notice bridal magazines on a table in the living room. Jane is thinking about being a bride, but you don't know who's in the lead to be the groom. In Victor Jose's opinion, the Swarthmore suitor is in the lead. You think strategically. You remind her this is 1945, the year you announced as a sophomore at Cornell that you would marry her. That prediction was yours, not hers. When she still seems undecided, you suggest taking a walk.

"A walk?" she asks, as if it's a novel idea.

"One foot in front of the other," you say.

She shrugs and says, "OK."

It's a beautiful day. What could be more romantic than to take Jane to the place where you first met? In kindergarten. The Orchard School. Not the school itself but a field outside it, a pretty place to walk.

You walk and talk more, presenting your case, the life you would have together—the seven children you talked about, the books and the writing you both have dreamed about. Unlike the time you proposed a year ago when, you acted frantically, over the top, now you present your case calmly. You stop and sit down under a tree. It seems a poor tactic, but you take a little nap. Maybe you're just exhausted from the war, from being a prisoner, from nearly starving, and being beaten, and shoveling corpses into piles. A bell sounds from a distant church and you wake. You stand and take Jane's arm and start to walk again. One foot in front of the other. You don't have to walk much farther or talk much more before she stops and smiles.

"Yes," she says.

You give her a beautiful diamond ring that was once part of a two-diamond ring worn by your mother that she had made into two rings, one for you and one for your brother.

Jane goes back to Washington later in July to resign from her job, wrap up her work for the OSS, and pack up her apartment.

Here you are with your father and sister in the house in Williams Creek, hoping that your brother, Bernie, will be able to join you when his and his wife's new baby is healthy and settled. In the meantime, you start writing. You write about the war. You write essays and stories. You write humorous pieces you send to the *New Yorker* and short stories you send to the *Saturday Evening Post*. You start collecting rejection slips. You look up old friends like Ben Hitz, whom you ask to be the best man at your wedding. You see Uncle Alex, who is always fun and has a lot of connections. You tell him you're considering a job with a labor union. You have always been on the side of the underdog. You like the idea of helping people get better wages, better working conditions. Uncle Alex knows just the man to see.

Uncle Alex is a friend of Powers Hapgood, a famous labor leader and organizer. He is also a Harvard man, which is how your conservative uncle Alex happens to know him. Uncle Alex arranges a lunch for you and your father and himself with Powers Hapgood at Stegemeier's Restaurant in downtown Indianapolis.

It turns out you voted for Powers Hapgood's wife, Mary, as the Socialist candidate for vice-president, on the same ticket with Norman Thomas in the last election. You vote Socialist, believing it is for the good of the common man;

as a private in the US Infantry, you feel that you qualify as a common man.

Hapgood comes in looking like an ordinary Indiana guy in a cheap business suit with a union pin on the lapel. He is friendly and fresh from a day in court, telling stories of his own experience on picket lines and as a labor leader, defending laboring men. Hapgood says the judge encouraged his stories of labor organizing, which included spending time in jail. The judge asked why Hapgood, a Harvard man and member of a good Indianapolis family, would involve himself in picket lines and labor organizing. Hapgood's response, with a smile, was "Why, the Sermon on the Mount, sir."

This reminds you of Ida Young and her telling you about the importance of the Sermon on the Mount. You especially remember the part that says, "Blessed are the merciful, for they shall find mercy."

The two things you quote most often throughout your work are the Sermon on the Mount and these words of your fellow Hoosier Eugene V. Debs, who ran for president as a Socialist: "As long as there is a lower class, I am in it. As long as there is a criminal class I am of it. As long as there is a soul in prison, I am not free."

You call these words "a moving echo of the Sermon on the Mount."

* * *

You are married in September in the backyard of Jane's house by an officiant of the Quaker faith, the faith of her family. It's probably the faith most compatible with your own family's freethinker/humanist tradition. The Quakers don't have any priests or ministers or rituals; they simply gather in silence until someone is moved to speak of what is in their mind and heart. The Quakers were the most active participants in helping slaves escape to freedom in Canada, acting as "conductors" on the Underground Railroad. You admire them.

The perfect place for your honeymoon is Lake Maxinkuckee. Your father has sold the family's house there, but the new owner gives you permission to use it for your honeymoon. The old rowboat is still at the dock, and it still has the name that's a combination of your brother's, your sister's, and yours: the *Beralikur*. This is the boat your brother and sister rowed while you swam behind it in your conquest of Lake Maxinkuckee. It's leaky but still afloat. Jane says you have to read *The Brothers Karamazov* by Fyodor Dostoevsky, which she thinks is the greatest novel of all time. She brings a copy with her so you can read it on your honeymoon.

You go off to Fort Riley, Kansas, where you serve the last three months of your enlistment as a clerk-typist. This assignment gives you time to write your own stories. You are very enthusiastic about your writing, and you take time to tell Jane how you feel about it in long impassioned letters that combine your love of Jane and love of writing. You send her the stories you write and the rejection letters you receive, and she responds with great enthusiasm. She sends you a wonderful letter singing high praise to your writing, comparing your work to that of the great Russian short story writer Anton Chekhov. She sounds like a young girl delirious with love, but she is delirious with your writing. Jane believes more than you do that someday you will be a great writer. Her enthusiasm is in some ways intimidating. What if you can't live up to it? You have to wonder—will she still love you if you don't turn out to be Shakespeare?

But Jane does not change her high opinion of your talent. She responds to a magazine advertisement for a writer's consultant named Scammon Lockwood. He says he can get new authors to editors and publishers and will read writing samples for free. Lockwood recommends writing to entertain the reader. His services, however, are not free, and you and Jane are not in a position to pay for them.

You get home from Fort Riley on December 1. Your career ambitions swing from labor unions to writing a letter offering your services to General Motors. After a discussion you have with Jane, you decide to use the GI Bill to go study anthropology at the University of Chicago. You don't want to be a professional anthropologist; you don't want to be a professor of anthropology. You want to use anthropology as a foundation for your writing, to give you a deeper understanding of culture and people. You consider anthropology to be a kind of poetry of science. Jane, in her pursuit of Russian literature, is on a scholarship to study Slovak languages.

* * *

To supplement your income, and also to draw on the excitement you have always felt about writing for newspapers, you sign on with the City News Bureau of Chicago. You say it's a "cocky operation." It's where everyone starts if they want to write for a Chicago newspaper. The news bureau supplies all the city papers with stories. You start out as a copyboy, just waiting for somebody to move on so you can become a reporter.

One Sunday you are there in the office, and you hear the police radio. You hear that in an office building three blocks over, a guy has just been killed in an elevator accident. There is nobody else to go, so you go over. You get there as soon as the fire department and police. The top of the elevator came down and crushed the elevator operator. You see the guy squashed and dead.

You phone the story in and the editor says, "OK, what did his wife say? Call up his wife."

"I can't do that," you say.

"Yes, you can."

You think it's dishonorable, but you do it. That's your job.

As a reporter, you go to police station after police station after police station, call on firehouses, and then go and call the coast guard. "Anything going on?" you ask. For eight hours you'll be on the South Side, the North Side, the West Side. You are looking around for everything. You can do at City News Bureau what you can't do afterward, which is walk into any part of town and start talking to people about their lives. You are outlaws. Some of you carry guns. One time you find a body.

You write in a letter to your cousin Walter about one of your most spectacular stories: "I covered a case last week wherein a woman of 54 (Mrs. Sosnowski) sawed her husband (Anthony) into two-foot lengths, and carried his segmented mortal remains a distance of nine blocks and threw them into the river. She had to make several trips. 'He died like a dog; now I'll die like a dog,' she said. 'I'm glad he's dead, the dog.'"

You are excited by the stories every beginning writer knows about Ernest Hemingway starting out on the *Kansas City Star* and by H. L. Mencken's descriptions of his adventures as a reporter for the *Baltimore Sun*. You have to get everything exactly right. You chase murders and car crashes and poor weather. You write about a man who died when his hand got stuck in an elevator. You earn twenty-seven dollars a week. You say, "Doing that job, surviving it, was like getting a Purple Heart. I wouldn't have missed it for anything."

Despite the low pay, the City News Bureau of Chicago gives you the experience mythologized in movies like *The Front Page*, movies that glamorize the role of the hard-bitten police reporter, the tough guy managing editor, the teletype machines banging out news from around the world, and the clack of the big clumsy Smith Coronas and Royal typewriters, the tools of your trade. One of the big Hollywood producers famously dismissed writers as "schmucks with Smith Coronas." For reporters, the type-writer was a badge of honor.

Like Hemingway, you learn that beauty and eloquence can be conveyed in short sentences. You say, "The point is to write as much as you know as quickly as possible." You learn to write opening sentences that summarize the most important facts.

You learn to write a story so someone can cut it without even reading it. You put all the important stuff in the beginning.

* * *

You are going to your classes at the University of Chicago Anthropology Department, and you're most fascinated by the lectures of Robert Redfield, who speaks about a certain kind of society called a "folk society" where people have a sense of belonging and group solidarity. It reminds you of the old group of Vonnegut families that assembled in summers at Lake Maxinkuckee when you were growing up.

Jane becomes pregnant in September and gives notice that she's leaving her scholarship and her studies at the University of Chicago. Like most wives do at this time, she puts her husband before any professional work of her own. She now devotes her time to domestic responsibilities and to editing your stories. You pride yourself on the fact that, unlike many married writers, you don't require Jane to type up your manuscripts. Hoping to be fair in adhering to your share of domestic responsibilities now that Jane is pregnant, you compose a contract of your and her duties and responsibilities.

***

CONTRACT between KURT VONNEGUT, JR. and JANE C. VONNEGUT, effective as of Sunday, January 26, 1947.

I, Kurt Vonnegut, Jr., that is, do hereby swear that I will be faithful to the commitments hereunder listed:

I. With the agreement that my wife will not nag, heckle, or otherwise disturb me on the subject, I promise to scrub the bathroom and kitchen floors once a week, on a day and hour of my own choosing. Not only that, but I will do a good and thorough job, and by that she means that I will get *under* the bathtub, *behind* the toilet, *under* the sink, *under* the icebox, *into* the corners; and I will pick up and put in some other location whatever movable objects happen to be on said floors at the time so as to get under them too, and not just around them. Furthermore, while I am undertaking these tasks I will refrain from indulging in such remarks as "Shit," "Goddamn sonofabitch," and similar vulgarities, as such language is nerve-wracking to have around the house when nothing more drastic is taking place than the facing of Necessity. *If I do not live up to this agreement*, my wife is to feel free to nag, heckle, and otherwise disturb me until I am driven to scrub the floors anyway—*no matter how busy I am*.

II. I furthermore swear that I will observe the following minor amenities:

a. I will hang up my clothes and put my shoes in the closet when I am not wearing them;

b. I will not track dirt into the house needlessly, by such means as not wiping my feet on the mat outside and wearing my bedroom slippers to take out the garbage;

c. I will throw such things as used-up match folders, empty cigarette packages, the piece of cardboard that comes in shirt collars, etc., into a wastebasket instead of leaving them around on chairs or the floor;

d. After shaving I will put my shaving equipment back in the medicine closet;

e. In case I should be the direct cause of a ring around the bathtub after taking a bath, I will, with the aid of Swift's Cleanser and a brush, *not* my washcloth, remove said ring;

Marriage and Chicago

f. With the agreement that my wife collects the laundry, places it in a laundry bag, and leaves the laundry bag in plain sight in the hall, I will take said laundry to the Laundry not more than three days after said laundry has made its appearance in the hall; I will furthermore bring the laundry back from the Laundry within two weeks after I have taken it;

g. When smoking I will make every effort to keep the ashtray I am using at the time upon a surface that does not slant, sag, slope, dip, wrinkle, or give way upon the slightest provocation; such surfaces may be understood to include stacks of books precariously mounted on the edge of a chair, the arms of the chair that has arms, and my own knees;

h. I will not put out cigarettes upon the sides of, or throw ashes into, either the red leather wastebasket or the stamp wastebasket that my loving wife made me for Christmas, 1945, as such practice noticeably impairs the beauty and ultimate practicability of said wastebaskets;

i. In the event that my wife makes a request of me, and that request cannot be regarded as other than reasonable and wholly within the province of a man's work (when his wife is pregnant, that is), I will comply with said request within three days after my wife has presented it. It is understood that my wife will make no reference to the subject, other than saying thank you, of course, within these three days; if, however, I fail to comply with said request after a more substantial length of time has elapsed, my wife shall be completely justified in nagging, heckling, or otherwise disturbing me until I am driven to do that which I should have done;

j. An exception to the above three-day time limit is the taking out of the garbage, which, as any fool knows, had better not wait that long; I will take out the garbage within three hours after the need for disposal has been pointed out to me by my wife. It would be nice, however, if, upon observing the need for disposal with my own two eyes, I should perform this particular task upon my own initiative, and thus not make it necessary for my wife to bring up a subject that is moderately distasteful to her;

k. It is understood that, should I find these commitments in any way unreasonable or too binding upon my freedom, I will take steps to amend them by counterproposals, constitutionally presented and politely discussed, instead of unlawfully terminating my obligations with a simple burst of obscenity, or something like that, and the subsequent persistent neglect of said obligations;

l. The terms of this contract are understood to be binding up until that time after the arrival of our child (to be specified by the doctor) when my wife will once again be in full possession of all her faculties, and able to undertake more arduous pursuits than are now advisable.

In the midst of her own household duties, Jane edits and makes suggestions for your essay "Wailing Shall Be in All Streets," which gets a response from Charles Angoff, editor of the *American Mercury*. He doesn't publish that essay but invites you to submit other work. You write a story called "Brighten Up" about prisoners of war and a savvy soldier who uses his street smarts to profit from his fellow prisoners. Your "war stories" are never about combat, because you feel that stories of combat encourage some people to think that shooting and fighting and blood and gore are glamorous, which leads them to want to engage in it. You tell Mr. Angoff you knew a soldier who behaved just like the character in your story. He doesn't publish it.

In the spring of 1947, you write a forty-page proposal for a thesis comparing nineteenth-century Native American mythologies to the work of the cubist painters of Paris. The thesis committee rejects the proposal as "too ambitious." Later that summer you propose another thesis idea—"The Mythologies of North American Nativistic Movements." They accept that as a subject, but it will probably take six months to come up with a formal proposal for it. In a letter to your cousin Walter Vonnegut, on September 1, 1947, you say, "Things are in one hell of a state of flux. Last night, we had our anniversary celebration at Jacques, a magnificent clip joint where one may live beyond his means under the stars in a flagstone courtyard. . . . We have run out of money, so it may be some time before I can complete the thesis. It seems expedient that I make some sort of economic adjustment as soon as possible."

The best of your opportunities comes from General Electric (GE). Better than the one at the *Dayton Journal*, better than the one at Bobbs-Merrill publishing company in Indianapolis. You and Jane decide you don't want to go back to live in your hometown of Indianapolis, because it would suck you into social obligations you want to avoid. Jane's mother is in the Junior League, and Jane would be expected to join, drawing the two of you into country club life.

Your brother, Bernie, has become a star scientist at GE, and they want to hire a reporter who can pitch stories about their new products and research to mass media markets. What a relief it will be to not have to scrimp and save for a while and enjoy a good salary! One of the requirements for working as a publicist at GE is to have a college degree. You tell them you have a master's degree in anthropology from the University of Chicago. You don't actually have it yet, but you fully intend to complete the work and earn the degree. GE doesn't check. You get the job.

6.

MAN IN A GRAY FLANNEL SUIT
(WITH SNEAKERS)

Your brother, Bernard, and his wife, Bow, and their first child live in a suburb of Schenectady, New York, which is GE's headquarters. The town they live in is called Alplaus. On October 15, you write to your father:

Dear Pop:

Your eldest son has treated your youngest like a prince. God bless him for that. I own a home now. Albeit humble, it's ours, and we'll love it I'm sure. And it's not so humble as the $7000 I'm paying for it. I'm selling 2 ½% bonds to get the money. I want no debt. This is the cheapest way for me to finance our home, and no recession can take it from us. It's a good little house, well built, and pleasant to see. Please come soon to examine it at your leisure. . . .

I have received a cordial letter from the Anthropology Department at Chicago, saying that I may take my master's finals at whatever eastern university I choose. I shall probably have the examinations, ten hours of them, proctored by Bernard's tenant, Bob Finholt of Union. That will be in December, I think. The thesis is another matter. It will take a while longer. I'm hoping to be sent to New York on business so I can do work in the Columbia Library. . . .

I left the middle west for Schenectady because the General Electric company offered me a more congenial, better paying job than did anyone else. And, as Allie and Jim were quick to perceive, people like us cannot afford to live in Indianapolis. Maybe we'll come back some day—but not now. I think we'll do a more honest job of living away from what will always be home.

I like my job. I'm not sorry that I took it, for it's better than I expected. It has an agreeable dignity to it, and demands of me a certain craftsmanship in which I can take pride. That, you'll agree, is important. Moreover, I'm earning, for the first time, enough to support my wife and child. And I'll have the will and the time and energy to write what I please when my work is done.

The house is a cozy two-bedroom cottage on a creek, beneath tall pine trees—it's a good place to write when you're home from work, at night and on weekends.

From nine to five, you work in the public relations department of GE. You pitch stories about their products and research to newspapers and magazines. At night and on weekends, you work at a table set up in the upstairs hallway. This is where you are going to write your thesis. You intend to do more research on it when you go to New York on business assignments and can take advantage of the library at Columbia. When you sit down at the typewriter at home, though, your good intentions to work on your thesis keep getting pushed aside by story ideas.

You keep writing stories and sending them off to magazines, undeterred by the fact that they keep coming back with rejection slips. You put aside war stories and start writing stories of everyday life of middle-class people, of families and of young men and women. You write a sensitive, credible story called "City" about a young man and woman meeting on a bus. Jane loves it and feels sure one of the women's magazines will take it. They don't. You keep writing.

Every weekday before you take the bus into Schenectady, you write, working on stories for an hour or so. Then you must put on your costume. To go to work at this great corporation, you must wear a suit and tie and a hat with a brim called a fedora and polished serious black shoes. As a grad student and a reporter, you didn't have to wear that kind of costume. You just wore sweaters and jackets and khakis and sneakers and joked with your buddies about the fedoras that your fathers wore, which you referred to as a "man's hat." You must put on the businessman costume to go to work five days a week at the corporation. You are sort of like Superman in reverse—when you come home, you take off the costume and continue your real work of writing stories.

In this new era after World War II, when more people in the United States work at white-collar jobs than on farms for the first time in US history, there is great fascination with corporations like General Electric, General Mills, General Motors, Kodak, Time Inc., Prudential, Citibank. Soon there will be books warning against the consequences of working "womb to tomb" at one of these big corporations like GE and getting the gold watch at retirement—books like *The Organization Man* and *The Lonely Crowd, Life in the Crystal Palace,* and novels like *The Man in the Gray Flannel Suit.* Will such a lifetime in the corporate office numb the senses, promote conformity, and take the spontaneity and fun out of life and work?

Not for you—though a practical joke you play in your early days at GE nearly costs you your job.

Uncle Alex sees a picture of Bernard in a story from the paper in Schenectady that was syndicated and published in Indianapolis. Alex writes to GE and asks for a copy of the picture that accompanies that story about Bernard's accomplishments. The paper sends Alex's letter to the GE News Bureau, and that's where you work, so you answer Uncle Alex's letter, thinking he will know you are kidding and knows you are working at GE. You make your response funny, feeling sure he will get the joke.

General Electric Company

Dear Mr. Vonnegut:

Mr. Edward Themak, city editor for the *Schenectady Gazette,* has referred your letter of November 26th to me.

The photograph of General Electric's Dr. Bernard Vonnegut originated from our office. However, we have no more prints in our files, and the negative is in the hands of the United States Signal Corps. Moreover, we have a lot more to do than piddle with penny-ante requests like yours.

We do have some other photographs of the poor man's Steinmetz, and I may send them to you in my own sweet time. But do not rush me. "Wee bit proud," indeed! Ha! Vonnegut! Ha! This office made your nephew, and we can break him in a minute—like an eggshell. So don't get in an uproar if you don't get the pictures in a week or two.

Also—one dollar to the General Electric Company is as the proverbial fart in a wind storm. Here it is back. Don't blow it all in one place.

Very truly yours,
Press Section
Guy Fawkes: GENERAL NEWS BUREAU

Guy Fawkes is the name of a seventeenth-century Englishman who threatened to blow up the Houses of Parliament—though his reputation has evolved from anarchist to the point that he's now thought of as more of a prankster than a bomb thrower. There is even a Guy Fawkes Day in England, when pranks are pulled, sort of like April Fools' Day.

Uncle Alex has never heard of Guy Fawkes, and he is spitting mad. He doesn't know you are working for GE. He consults a lawyer, but before any action is taken, Uncle Alex is informed that you—who started telling jokes as a kid at the dinner table—are now working for the news bureau of GE. Uncle Alex calms down, but he never brings the incident up with you, and you don't mention it either. He saves the letter, though, and later gives it to Bernie.

Even though you get past the Guy Fawkes prank with your family, your boss, George Griffin, does not appreciate your humor. GE is not a producer of sophomoric jokes, nor is GE's stationery to be used for pranks.

You escape the doghouse by proving your worth as a serious publicist when you pitch a story about GE products to the *New York Times* and they use it, which shows the company was smart to hire a man with newspaper experience. Your ability to nose out news of GE products and place it in the press (as well as your brother's importance to the company) probably saves you (this time). Better watch your step! Boss Griffin is a dedicated organization man, and GE is a proud giant of an organization. It makes everything from rotor blades for jet engines and turbines for powerful dams in the US and abroad to washing machines, refrigerators, and toasters for the home. GE names itself the "House of Magic" and proudly proclaims, "Progress is our most important product."

GE takes care of its workers too. The massive campus not only has scientific laboratories and offices but also provides comfort for its employees, from a restaurant and medical clinic to a baseball diamond and athletic club. There's a summer camp that outdoes anything the Boy Scouts have come up with, including rival "teams" with their own names and colors and pep songs.

The gray flannel atmosphere is broken every Monday morning when the dress code is relaxed and publicists are allowed to come in wearing sneakers, shirts without ties, even without jackets, to meet with the boss. The boss is a former army officer who your buddies say delights in picking apart your appearance, riding you for coming in during the other days of the week without a tie or a jacket, wearing your sneakers and maybe corduroys instead of regulation slacks or suit pants. He can't fire you, because you are good at your job, successfully pitching stories to magazines as well as newspapers about the terrific exploits of GE (you have a big one with photographs coming out in *Life*, a major coup). Still the boss rides you, singling you out at every opportunity for some violation of the dress code. It's almost as if the bullies show up at every stage of your life: the jocks stuffing you in a trash can in high school; "Junior," the kid Nazi, tormenting you with a bayonet in Dresden; and now the corporation boss picking you as his favorite new young publicist to pick on. You didn't crack at the point of Junior's bayonet, and you don't crack at the boss's barbs.

Whether from your work in anthropology courses at Chicago or covering stories for the City New Bureau or finding out what the GE research lab is up to in your job pitching the company's products to newspapers and magazines, you are also filing away material for possible stories of your own. You get ideas not only from new work being developed at the research lab but also from going to parties of GE scientists with your brother, Bernie.

At one of those parties, you are interested to hear that H. G. Wells, one of the early science-fiction writers (this worldwide-bestselling English author's books include *The War of the Worlds*, *The First Men in the Moon*, and *In the Days of the Comet*), once paid a visit to General Electric, and GE's scientific star, Irving Langmuir, gave Wells an idea for a story. What if there was a way to make water solid at room temperature? That could cause an apocalypse, an end to life on Earth. Wells didn't express interest in the idea, but you do. At a party for GE scientists and their wives, you ask a scientist who's an expert in crystallography if it's possible that water could be turned into ice at room temperature. The scientist is intrigued enough to go off to a corner by himself and try to think it out. After a while he comes back and tells you that it isn't possible. You thank him, but the idea of such a possibility stays in your head.

In the meantime, a tidal wave of new rejection slips washes into your mailbox at home, and rather than becoming discouraged, you become more determined. Your pals at GE, like Ollie Lyon, a war veteran like you, and Bob Pace, a Shortridge High School grad and another vet, realize you have more discipline than your fellow dreamers—the ones who say "someday" they are going to write stories for magazines—and they don't even bother to invite you out on weekends, knowing you are working on stories then and respecting your commitment.

The latest batch of stories that have been rejected, aimed at the best women's magazines—*McCall's, Cosmopolitan, Redbook*—have been no more successful than the batch before about soldiers whom you don't send into battle. It occurs to you that you are sitting in the midst of another universe of story ideas—GE may be not only a source of subjects for news stories for papers and magazines but also a universe of short-story ideas sprung from science. You are not thinking of it as science fiction, since the magazines that publish that brand of writing don't pay enough to match the blood, sweat, and tears you put into your stories. A penny a word wouldn't keep your family in cereal for a day, while markets like the popular weeklies—*Collier's*, the *Saturday Evening Post*, and the like—reward writers with twenty-five times that, which would provide meat and potatoes for your growing flock—Mark and Edie, with Nanny on the way, and remember your and Jane's pledge of seven!

You feel "Mnemonics" and "Report on the Barnhouse Effect" are real winners. You believe they are worthy of being represented by New York literary agents, whose prestige will give the stories a greater shot at selling.

7.

BREAKTHROUGH

In your hallway-alcove office, you finish writing "The Barnhouse Effect," a story you think is your best, and you send it with a few others to Russell & Volkening, an agency that represents some of the top writers of the time (like Saul Bellow, on his way to a Nobel Prize). You get a letter back from Diarmuid Russell with a few nice words about your stories (he says they are "brisk"), but he fears that they won't go over well with editors. At least he suggests that you send "The Barnhouse Effect" to *Collier's* and the *Saturday Evening Post*. OK, if Russell makes a suggestion, you take it.

Writers hungry for publication scan each letter or note of rejection for any hint of encouragement. They read any scrawled comments made on the standard printed rejection like scholars poring over the Dead Sea Scrolls. When "The Barnhouse Effect" comes back from *Collier's* in April, you read the penciled message at the bottom of the rejection form with eager attention. The scrawl says, "This is a bit sententious for us. You're not the Kurt Vonnegut who worked on the *Cornell Sun* in 1942, are you?"

The signature is undecipherable to you. You file the document in the manila envelope you keep for stories, with date submitted, returned, and submitted elsewhere. No flash of lightning illuminates the mysterious moniker. It's more than two months later when you run into a photographer named George Burns who you sometimes work with on stories for the news bureau. You confess you are spending most of your non-GE time writing stories and sending them out to magazines—so far, with no luck. The photographer, a fellow veteran, says he worked on the army magazine *Yank* with a guy who is now an editor at *Collier's*. You should send something to him, Burns says—his name is Knox Burger. You hurry home and get out the *Collier's* rejection and decipher the scrawled signature as "Knox Burger." You remember him from Cornell—while you worked on the *Sun*, he was an editor of the humor magazine the Cornell *Widow*. You cook up an assignment for yourself in New York and write to Knox from Alplaus, NY on June 24th, 1949:

> Dear Knox:
>
> George Burns, who, never having read anything of mine, takes a casual interest in my writing career, allowed as how he had a friend on *Collier's* fiction staff who might be able to give me some help. The friend turned out to be you.

This information cleared up a mystery of several months' standing—a not wholly unjust pencil message on the bottom of a rejection slip: "This is a little sententious for us. You're not the Kurt Vonnegut who worked on the *Cornell Sun* in 1942, are you?" It was signed by Owen Buyer, Orme Bruyes, or Dunk Briges, all persons unknown to me.

In reply to your question: yes, I am the Kurt Vonnegut. I am glad to know that you are the Knox Burger, and that you are doing so well for yourself.

Sorry you didn't care for the story. I got a typewritten letter back on it from the *Post*. *Story* has now had it for a month. You're right. It was a dog. . . .

I plan to be in New York Tuesday and Wednesday of next week. What are the chances of having lunch with you?

Yours truly,

Kurt Vonnegut

***

Knox sends you a telegram three days later telling you to call when you get to New York. You hit it off with him, a man your own age who is sharp, tough-minded, and a good talker.

After your meeting with Knox, you go home and send him a selection of stories. Knox responds to the story "Mnemonics":

Dear Kurt:

Here is "Mnemonics" by Mark Harvey, as pompous a pseudonym as any that I have encountered.

I think we might be able to take this one if you do some more work on it. I could give you another page to work with, and in those twenty-five lines, you will somehow have to strengthen your point so that the people in the provinces will have an unmistakable awareness that this man is happy because he indulges himself in sadistic daydreams. The reason this has to be made more obvious is that while I am sure it has overtones of universality, it is a little clinical and so morbid that many people will not want to believe that is the point of this story.

Perhaps you can give the Mnemonics course a little more description, incorporating the general approach of how pictures aid memory and the fact that different people have different fantasies. Perhaps the teacher of the course could cite some extremely pleasant and innocuous fantasy for the purpose of contrast, and you could have your protagonist somehow feel more at home with fantasies of another kind. In other words, the significance of the various horrors that aid his memory has to be laid on thicker. And yet I don't want you to make this story too obviously bald or make your point didactically. Maybe the last fantasy, in which the matches are dragged in, is a little weak. Couldn't it be something connected more intrinsically with the office? Another thing, to include his wife in these terrible fantasies seems a little thick, and for the purpose of contrast, you might have her stir in him a pleasant image—or whether or not you leave her in as she is, you might contrast the image her request evokes by another image inspired by a very pleasant secretary. Maybe that would give you trouble, though.

Incidentally, you might devote a line to bolstering the fact that this fictional memory course is based on actual techniques used in such courses.

At any rate, I honestly think the thing has possibilities, and I hope you can find ways to bring it off for us.

Sincerely,

Knox Burger

You immediately get to work in your hallway office, revising each morning before you take the bus to the GE campus to follow through on all of Knox's suggestions. You send off the new version to Knox and get a letter back in response on July 19.

Dear Kurt,

I seem to be sending "Mnemonics" back for further revisions. I have my earlier letter to you, at hand, but I suspect it was probably fatuous. I should never try to dictate these things.

You have incorporated the background stuff on Mnemonics very well into the beginning of the story. However, I am still leery of having readers too thoroughly outraged and disgusted with Alfred. He needs sympathy. . . . I hope you have not lost patience with me, and I will keep my fingers crossed.

By the way, I hope you do not mind, but I have given your name to a literary agent, my former boss here, Kenneth Littauer. He is a very good man, and I told him that I thought you might turn out to be a skillful and prolific writer.

Sincerely,

Knox Burger

Knox's suggestions about the story are quite specific. Knox says that the character Alfred needs to be more motivated and suggests how to do that. He suggests that a wife's shopping list be more imaginative and even gives examples of items she could be shopping for.

Years later, you will say, "Agents and editors back then could tell a writer how to fine-tune a story as though they were pit mechanics and the story were a racecar." Many young writers would be discouraged by this new set of instructions and either give up or make an angry reply, but you are not like most young writers. You are determined to make this work. It's as if you've been fishing for years without catching anything, and now you have something on the line, and you are not going to let it go. You write back to Knox on July 21:

Dear Knox:

"Many hands make much work light."—old Chinese proverb.

Perhaps MNEMONICS, enclosed for the third time, will meet your needs. If it doesn't, God knows you're blameless. I am in receipt of reasonable instructions from you, which are at least as long as the story itself.

I think I've made the hero likable.

I think I've made the two villains, Alfred's wife and Alfred's boss, terrible enough to deserve just about anything they get in his mnemonic daydreams.

Kurt Vonnegut

You await Knox's response. It comes on his *Collier's* stationery on August 1.

Dear Kurt:

I have some bad news for you. We are not going to take MNEMONICS. I wasn't entirely satisfied with the revision, but that was really no fault of yours. Nonetheless, I passed it onto the publisher, as I do all doubtful or contentious stories, and he feels that "It doesn't come off. . . . The net result lacks conviction. It just leaves a bad taste in your mouth."

Needless to say, I'm very sorry, but I do feel that you will be able to write for us, and please don't be discouraged.

Sincerely,

Knox Burger

Knox can't continue giving detailed instructions to one unpublished author when he has to edit the many writers who contribute the four stories that *Collier's* magazine publishes every week. He's done you a great favor by recommending you to the literary agent Kenneth Littauer, at Littauer & Wilkinson. Littauer was fiction editor of *Collier's* before Knox Burger. In World War I, Littauer was a pilot in the Lafayette Escadrille, a volunteer air force for the French Army. As an editor and then an agent, he is a colorful figure in New York City, wearing a bowler hat and carrying a furled umbrella. Max Wilkinson previously worked for the movie company MGM, and his claim to fame is that the author F. Scott Fitzgerald once punched him in the mouth. You could not have created better characters to be your agents than the real Littauer and Wilkinson.

You are happy to have a literary agent, and you send your story "The Barnhouse Effect" to Kenneth Littauer. He responds with one of those Knox-like lists of suggestions. It's as if he is the new mechanic fixing your race car. You write to him with gratitude on September 28:

> Dear Mr. Littauer:
>
> I was very pleased to find out how THE BARNHOUSE EFFECT really ended. I wouldn't unguild you the lily for anything. You write real good.
>
> I feel odd and grateful for having had you take me by the hand from title to punchline on this opus. It's a pretty amazing service Littauer & Wilkinson offer, and one I hope to need less and less as time goes on.

I've junked everything you returned to me and am beginning some fresh stories. I hope to have the first of these in your hands within a month. A prospective novel is pretty well outlined but I don't intend to start work on it until (when and if) I sell a few shorts. Sorry you and Knox were revolted by ENTERPRISE. My wife and I were too, but after checking *REDBOOK*, etc., we mistakenly supposed that it was the sort of thing magazines of that sort ran. A dog. I won't try that again.

Yours truly,

Kurt Vonnegut Jr.

At the end of October, you come home from a hard day at the GE office and find an envelope that Jane has put on the piano with a check for $675—which was $750 before the 10 percent agent fee.

On October 28, 1949, you write to your father.

Dear Pop:

I sold my first story to *Collier's*. Received my check ($750 minus a 10% agent's commission [from the Littauer & Wilkinson Agency]) yesterday noon. It now appears that two more of my works have a good chance of being sold in the near future.

I think I'm on my way. I've deposited my first check in a savings account, and, as and if I sell more, will continue to do so until I have the equivalent of one year's pay at G.E.

Four more stories will do it nicely, with cash to spare (something we never had before). I will then quit this goddamn nightmare job, and never take another one so long as I live, so help me God.

I'm happier than I've been for a good many years.

Love.

K

Your father realizes this is a turning point for you. You have found your life's work. He glues the letter on a piece of masonite, and on the back he writes a quote from Shakespeare's *The Merchant of Venice*: "An oath, I have an oath in Heaven: Shall I lay perjury on my soul?"

You have a deeper oath to yourself than the one to be a writer—to make a living as a writer. Your experience in Dresden enabled you to know the senses, the smell, the touch, the feel of fabric in soldiers' winter underwear, the light, the way it slants into a boxcar window, the stink of another man you slept next to for days—all these are things which can't be known except by being there; except by what Walt Whitman meant when he wrote "I am the man, I suffered, I was there."

You have found your life's mission. It will be with you as you write other stories, other books. This is your sword in the stone, your Holy Grail.

PART TWO

Your Life as a Writer

INTERLUDE

You start out as a writer making a precarious living by selling short stories to magazines. After I graduate from Columbia in 1955, I start out as a writer making a precarious living by selling articles to magazines. After eight years of racing to meet deadlines to pay the rent in New York City, I am awarded a Nieman Fellowship in Journalism in 1963, which takes me to Cambridge, Massachusetts, for a free year at Harvard, all expenses paid (sigh of relief!).

When I move to Cambridge, a Columbia College friend suggests I look up a lawyer there he knows named Fred Wiseman, who has started producing films. Little do I know that you wrote to Knox Burger in July to tell him that "an interesting young man named Fred Wiseman is optioning *Cat's Cradle* for a movie. . . . Do you know him? He's a lawyer who got hooked on films."

I've been reading your stories ever since I heard about you at Shortridge. I eagerly bought a copy of *Player Piano* when it came out, having recently read *Cat's Cradle*, which I notice in well-worn paperback editions stuck in the back pockets of college students all over Cambridge and Boston, where colleges abound.

Wiseman invites you and Jane to come up from the Cape to have dinner with him and his wife, and knowing that you are from Indianapolis, he also invites the two people from Indianapolis he knows who are living in the

Boston-Cambridge area—me and Kathy Kane, an up-and-coming legislator who will become a deputy mayor of Boston. You and I and Kathy Kane have something else in common: besides coming from Indianapolis, all of us went to Shortridge High School, and we all wrote for the Shortridge *Daily Echo*. This is like Old Home Week. I think of a rhyme from *Cat's Cradle*:

> *Nice, nice, very nice—*
> *So many different people*
> *In the same device.*

You have been an inspiration to me, a reassuring example that someone who went to my high school and wrote for the *Echo* can publish books and stories and "make it" as a writer (by "make it" I mean make a living at it). I am also impressed that you have published novels, for even though I have published enough articles to pay the rent and to write a journalistic book about the Puerto Ricans in New York (*Island in the City*), my dream is to write a novel. For writers of your generation and mine, the novel is the great dream.

Your writing is friendly and clear and conveys new ideas, new ways of looking at things that seem natural, unassuming, as if a friend is talking to you. Does it mean that you are like that too? I will soon find out.

On the night of the dinner at the Wisemans', you and

Jane are glowing. You seem happy to meet us, pleased to be in our company. You are tall, kind of shaggy, informal, comfortable. Jane is blonde and attractive in a warm, friendly way, like an ideal sister who understands you. We talk about Shortridge, and you confess that you didn't get along with "the sports gods"—you were skinny and gangly and felt uncoordinated. You never went out for any team. I tell how I had flat feet and was too slow to make the basketball team, but I figured I might become a distance runner, thinking I didn't have to be fast to run the mile—you couldn't sprint all that way! I trained, bought a stopwatch, and timed myself on the track. My time was 7:02, an embarrassment. I ran more practice miles around the high school track and tried again with the stopwatch. In fact, I had cut my time—but by only two seconds. My failure to break the seven-minute mile turned me away from running and to writing. You love this story. We have a bond—we both were failures at high school sports.

The talk turns to writing, and Jane beams as she speaks of your having "a magic year," and you smile and say, "That was the year that everything sold."

"Every story we sent out," Jane says, "came back with a check."

The first check—the payment for your story "Report on the Barnhouse Effect" —came in a blue envelope, Jane says. "And I set it on the piano so he would see it when he came home."

What a life! Living in Cape Cod and writing stories that are published in the most popular magazines and writing novels too! How could anyone imagine a better life? I have no idea, of course, what such a life is like, least of all what yours is like.

When I tell friends that I met you—you are just becoming known, with *Cat's Cradle*, *The Sirens of Titan*, *Mother Night*, and *Canary in a Cat House* all having come out within a few years—people eagerly ask me, "Did you talk about writing?"

"No," I say. "We talked about high school."

***

Looking back now from the vantage of a couple of decades into the twenty-first century, the era of your life then seems antiquated, limited in its entertainments, its communications. Names like "Facebook," "Instagram," and "Twitter" were not in the language; there was no "social media" because there was no internet. People spoke on rotary telephones affixed to the walls of their homes or offices. For real communication, to report the happenings of your life to a friend, you wrote a letter, either by writing in cursive script (a skill no longer taught in schools) with pencil or pen, or you composed your message on the keys of a typewriter, folded the paper you wrote on, placed it in an envelope you licked to seal shut, wrote the name and address of the person to whom you were sending it, stuck a US postage stamp in the upper right-hand corner, and dropped it in the nearest mailbox. Two or three or four days later (depending on the distance of its destination), the message would reach the person you were writing to; they would open it and read your latest news (only two or three days old or maybe four if you lived on a different coast). This was our Instagram, our Twitter!

I know this system by heart, and I describe it with a feeling of nostalgia and loss, since I grew up in your era too, Kurt, though I am ten years younger and still hanging onto the blue-green orb you loved and whose thoughtless desecration you lamented. I still stumble when using the computer, the internet, and my iPhone or texting with the speed of a turtle.

I edited a whole book called Kurt Vonnegut: Letters, so I know how you loved writing letters and how important they were to you, as they were to all of us before the era of emails and tweets. (Will there now be books of writers' emails published to tell their life stories? Emails and tweets seem closer to the telegram-like communications of the Tralfamadorians of Slaughterhouse-Five than letters.)

Unlike the Tralfamadorians, you and I are both letter-writing animals, so it seemed to me a good idea to use some of your letters as a kind of "skeleton" of the story of this part of your life, reminding me and the readers of where you were and how you felt about it.

8.

TAKING THE LEAP

A few days after your first published short story, "Report on the Barnhouse Effect," appears in *Collier's*, you write to your old Cornell friend Miller Harris, whose father owns the Arrow Shirt Company. Harris, who was your mentor when he was editor of the *Cornell Daily Sun*, is also writing short stories, as well as working at his father's company.

February 16th, 1950
Alplaus, New York

Dear Miller,

Since my father is a poor but honest architect, I don't have a shirt factory. I do have a wife and two kids, though. So I work for General Electric, writing publicity for them. . . .

It is a terrible job, so writing stories for a living is a very attractive notion. It's possible that I'll be able to make the grade in the next year. God, I sure hope so. In which case, I will, of course, write a novel about G.E. It'd be about 20th

Century Man, proving that he is happy—and that the glum people, like us, are a pathetic and noisy minority who write.
. . .

Since seeing you last, I have been an A.S.T.P. engineer, an infantryman, a P.O.W. in Germany, a graduate student of anthropology (sea shells) at Chicago, a police reporter in Chicago, and now a public relations man. (How the hell are you, you old sonofagun. Cigarette? Martini?)

You write again to Harris with what will be the first of many ideas you will have in the coming years to make extra money to supplement your income from writing. You write to him on February 28, 1950.

Dear Miller:

O.K., so people who want to write for a living are doomed to failure. I have other angles, about which this letter is.

This letter is to Harris the shirtmaker. I have a proposition for a man who can manufacture and market bowties. Can you? I know nothing about the garment trade, so perhaps the whole thing is preposterous.

Anyway, I have an idea for a bowtie. If you heard this idea, I think you would agree that it would be a sensational teen-ager fad for a few wild, lucrative weeks.

Does this sort of thing interest you? The tie would cost virtually nothing to make—no mechanical gadgets, no wires, no electronic tubes. It's just a plain, ordinary bowtie (no, it doesn't glow in the dark, dammit), put together like any other bowtie. But there is one thing about it that would make it a natural for promotion.

Are you interested? If you are, and if the idea is any good, how will you reward me?

Kurt

You succeed in the goal you conveyed to your father to have the equivalent of a year's salary at GE saved from your writing by the year's end, which you accomplish by selling two more stories to *Collier's*. You also begin your first novel, which grows out of your experience working at GE. The novel reflects the new machinery that is making automation a key element of American life. You also have fun satirizing the corporate world and your firsthand experience of "the man in the gray flannel suit." As you remark about the novel based on your experience at GE, "I bit the hand that fed me."

Your novel also makes use of the subject of your first thesis proposal in anthropology at the University of Chicago. The workers in the fictional city of Ilium, New York, transplant and update the Ghost Dance of the Plains Indians to serve as their own protest movement against the corporation. You always find ways to use what you learned in the past in other works. Nothing is wasted. You also work into the story a question from a visiting maharaja that underlies the fear of automation, assembly line work, and technology: "What are people for?"

In December, you write to GE that you will be leaving the company, effective January 1, 1951.

That summer, you take the family, which now includes daughter Edie and son Mark, to the town of Hyannis Port on Cape Cod. This is the psychic opposite of Alplaus, Schenectady, and the GE "campus." In contrast to corporate suburbia, Hyannis Port is more like Greenwich Village on the ocean. Art galleries, clubs, and coffeehouses line the street where it's "casual day" seven days a week, blessed by an ocean breeze. You and Jane love it—and so do your friends. That becomes a problem. There is a constant flow of visitors, and entertaining them takes up writing time. By September, you are telling people not to come—Jane even writes to her mother asking her *not* to visit her grandson and granddaughter yet.

You decide to sell your house in Alplaus and buy a house in the town of Osterville on Cape Cod. As you will later write Miller Harris on December 11, 1953, "I'm happy with Cape Cod. The place is loaded with romantics, who've fled the big cities, and they're all wise, in interesting and special ways. Me too."

You are able to finish your first novel, *Player Piano*, and your agents, Littauer and Wilkinson, negotiate a contract for it before Christmas. You and Jane start a Great Books course on the Cape, and the first book you read is the *Odyssey*; it gives you the idea for your first play, *Penelope*, about a hero coming home to his wife after years of adventure. You know that the great American playwright Eugene

O'Neill got his start on Cape Cod, when he and some other writers, artists, and intellectuals from Greenwich Village came to Provincetown in the summer of 1915 and started a theater company, putting on O'Neill's first works in a shanty on the Provincetown wharf. His play *Anna Christie* went on to Broadway and won the Pulitzer Prize, launching a career that made O'Neill the second American to win the Nobel Prize in Literature.

The theater company that O'Neill and his friends began lasted only two summers on the Cape, but the theater tradition is still alive there. You join the Orleans Theatre as well as the Barnstable Comedy Club, becoming involved as a volunteer fundraiser and actor as well as a playwright. You write to Knox Burger in a letter dated only "winter, 1951":

> My play is all finished. About 100 copies have been mailed out to famous actors. Apparently, I did O.K. on the revision. Now I'm back on short stories. They are cruel little bastards. I hate them. I will hear about the Guggenheim in early March [you applied for this fellowship in hopes of enabling a trip back to Dresden to refresh your memories for writing a novel about your experience there]. If I get it, I will finish up another play that's fairly close to being done right now.
>
> I sure do like plays. If *Penelope* goes over, I will have taken the giant step that will free me to write plays for the rest of my life. If not, I won't have taken the giant step. If not, so what? I am a nihilist.

Your play runs for a week at the Orleans Theatre. You write to Knox Burger again on April 12, 1952:

> I will go on writing short stories, and Littauer will go on showing them to you, and perhaps you'll go on finding some that fill your current needs. . . .
>
> I want more *Collier's* money, need more *Collier's* money, and will do my best to get it.
>
> It doesn't appear that I can go on much longer making a living as a short story writer. After the novel comes out, picking its way through beds of tender mores and folkways with the grace of a ballet dancer, I hope to get a job in Hollywood. I've got a wife and two kids, and have to do something that will bring in money steadily. . . .
>
> Just finished up page proofs on the book [Player Piano]. It'll be out in July, I hear.
>
> Jane and I will probably be in New York for a few days in May—at which time we'll come to see you.
>
> I should own a shirt factory. . . .
>
> I'd like to develop as a writer, but who's got the bar-bells and the gymnasium? . . .
>
> Yours truly,
>
> Kurt Vonnegut, Jr.

In the letter to Miller Harris from December 11, 1953, you write: "Jane and I did a dizzy thing a few days ago, and it turned out to be the best lark in years. We went to Harvard for two days. We just walked in and sat down in different classrooms, and nobody came around collecting tickets. . . . [They heard great professors lecture on painting, on the writers Hawthorne and Melville, on Supreme Court decisions.]"

* * *

Player Piano is published that summer to respectful but mixed reviews. The *New York Times* finds it "less serious" than *Brave New World* and wonders whether you are "a trustworthy prophet or not," but at least it calls you "a sharp-eyed satirist." The hemming and hawing of the reviews in general doesn't result in landslide sales (the printing was a modest 7,600), but your agents Littauer and Wilkinson have helped broaden your short fiction market, placing stories of yours in the *Saturday Evening Post*, *Redbook*, *Cosmopolitan*, and other well-paying magazines.

You foresee that television is replacing magazine fiction and even radio as the primary entertainment of Americans. TV gobbles up the advertising money that used to be spent in magazines. You observe to a friend that "My 'cash cows', the slick magazines, are dying off."

Collier's magazine is going from weekly to biweekly in 1953. They used to publish five short stories a week. In 1957, *Collier's* dies. You are looking for additional ways to support your family. You apply for a job teaching English at Cape Cod Community College. They turn you down.

Harry Brague, the editor you worked with on *Player Piano*, has given you a modest contract for a new novel. You have several ideas for novels in mind, and you tell him when you get one of them to one hundred pages, you will send it to him. On August 15, 1953, you write to him:

> Dear Harry:
>
> It's good of you to get me the $500. I'll try to pay it back, and I don't plan to ask for the second $500.
>
> The money will keep me in business here for a few more weeks, and the dream is that something extraordinarily nice will happen in that time. If something nice doesn't happen, then something terrible will happen. I'll have to get a job.

You get a job at an ad agency in Boston for seven months. You commute there from Cape Cod. Your novel, *Player Piano*, is reprinted as a selection of the Doubleday Science Fiction Book Club.

You write Harry Brague on February 7, 1954:

> I've squandered all my time on short stories and scripts that haven't sold, for the most part. It was a gamble worth taking—but, like most gambles, it didn't pay off. So I haven't got a book and I haven't got any money.
>
> Well, neither bitch is quite justified. I've got a little money left, and I've got a book going. It's going to be a good book, Harry. We're just all going to have to be patient. . . .

There's a good chance I'll finish this book this year. I want to finish it very much, and I'm busting to get at it and keep at it all day, every day. But I've got to earn that freedom with short stories.

The "lag time" between having stories accepted for publication and the arrival of the check has you always looking for ways to supplement your perilous income from writing.

You hear there is a job opportunity to write for a new Time Inc. magazine called *Sports Illustrated*. You go to New York to apply for the job.

The last time you took a test on your writing, you were a freshman at Cornell applying for a job on the *Cornell Daily Sun*. That was easy. You've known all the rules of journalism since working on the Shortridge *Daily Echo*. This is different. You have no idea what kind of writing the editors of a new sports magazine put out by Time Inc. are looking for.

You are sent to a bare room with a typewriter and paper and asked to write an article based on a clipping from a newspaper. The clipping reports that a horse at the Aqueduct Racetrack bolted when the starting gun was fired and jumped over the fence that enclosed the track. You read the article over several times and stare off into space. You wonder what the editors want from you. You take a piece of blank paper from the desk and roll it into the big Smith Corona typewriter. Should you make up a story about the horse being abducted by space aliens? You stare at the walls.

Taking the Leap

127

You sit and stand up and sit down again. You look at your watch. After an hour or so, you type this sentence: "The horse jumped over the fucking fence."

You put on your coat and go home.

You never hear from *Sports Illustrated*.

* * *

On May 11, 1954, you write Knox Burger:

> I bought a television set day before yesterday. Best sample of American enterprise I've seen since a young man sold me a subscription to all the Crowell-Collier publications five years ago. A guy came into my office (over the Osterville Package Store), and said, "It's about time you got television. You're going to have it by four this afternoon." He was a man in a genial mood to dicker, and he damn well wasn't going to leave without having made an offer I was bound to admit it was reasonable. Hey presto!. . .
>
> P.S. Have you read Aristotle's *Poetics?* I just did, and found in there everything any editor or writer ever told me about putting a story together. I couldn't think of a single amendment based on discoveries since 322 B.C. It's clear, and it isn't very long—and you might well recommend it to promising youngsters. Like me.
>
> Kurt

***

Your third child and second daughter, Nanette, arrives in October. You now have a family of five to feed, clothe, and shelter. To accommodate your larger family, you buy a new house, which you describe to Knox in a letter on October 26, 1954:

> We bought a big house in Barnstable. Two-hundred years old. View of the Barnstable dunes, and on a fresh water pond with some fish in it. Six fireplaces. This is probably the financial manipulation that will finish me. . .
> We won't move in until next spring. It's a better house than the one we were so hot about, and ten-thousand dollars cheaper. Six fireplaces. Plenty of guest rooms. A guest apartment, in fact.
> Six fireplaces.
> Kurt

***

Player Piano is reprinted in paperback by Bantam Books with the title *Utopia 14*.
You write to Harry Brague on November 30, 1954:

> Look, old friend, as a psychological device, let's pretend there isn't ever going to be another book written by me. Then one

bright day, into your office will come a manuscript, and we'll all be proud as Punch.

Honest to God—I don't think there's ever going to be another book, I can't imagine where the time is going, and I get sick if I think about it too much.

Hokay?

In Christ,

Kurt

On February 1, 1955, you write to Knox:

Now we own two houses. By God, I sure wish we didn't. Expensive. . . .

Jesus—wouldn't it be nice to write just one play a year, or just one anything?

I've pretty well pooped out as a hack. The old Moxie is gone. . . .

Everything's going to be just grand, though. Jane says so. She says she knows it in her bones. And I no kidding believe her.

You write to Knox again on October 25, 1955:

Right now I am faced with a typically New York problem, which is how to bring my mediocrity before the public. I've written a play which some people . . . think is screamingly funny, and which some people . . . say stinks. My life (at 33 years of age) hangs by a thread. That damn play has just got to be produced. Yet it looks like it won't be. . . .

Yours truly,

Kurt

* * *

With no prospects of cash coming in, you continue your efforts to find other ways of hitting the jackpot financially. On November 14, 1956, you write to Mr. Henry Saalfield of the Saalfield Game Company in Akron, Ohio, proposing a children's board game called HQ:

> Dear Mr. Saalfield:
>
> I am writing to you at the suggestion of your cousin and my neighbor, Mike Handy.
>
> I have invented a board game, which Mike has seen and seems to like. I have played the game about a thousand times, and it works like a dollar watch. The bugs are out of the rules.
>
> It is similar in mood to chess, and is played on a standard checkerboard. It has enough dignity and interest, I think, to become the third popular checkerboard game.

Your idea is turned down.

* * *

In 1957, you carry on your dream of playwriting, creating a stage adaptation of your short story "EPICAC" (*Collier's*, 1950), staged as part of an evening of one-act plays at the Barnstable Comedy Club. No one suggests you are following in the footsteps of the great Eugene O'Neill, but at least you got a play produced, even if only a one act.

Playwriting, like novel writing, has yet to pay off in a way that can support a family, and in a new effort to gain financial stability, you open the second dealership in America for the Saab Automobile company. Your Saab dealership has a showroom and garage on a road into town not far from your house. Most people in America are not yet familiar with the Swedish automobile, and you learn on the job about some of its quirks. If you leave a Saab parked for more than a day, the oil settles like maple syrup to the bottom of the gas tank. When you start it up, the exhaust could black out a whole neighborhood. One time, you black out the town of Woods Hole on Cape Cod. You are coughing like everybody else. You can't imagine where all the smoke has come from.

You bring your ten-year-old son, Mark, along with you when you take customers for a drive. You usually do the test driving while the prospective customer sits in the passenger seat. Mark tries to tell you not to go around corners so fast, especially if the customers are middle aged or older, but you think it's the best way to explain front-wheel drive. Some of the prospective customers are shaken and green at the end of the rides. Mark suggests that you just let the customers drive. You don't take his advice. You don't sell many cars. You open the dealership in the spring and close it in December.

* * *

Jane has been doing something you don't understand. She keeps gathering old clothes and blankets and putting them in the barn on your property that no one uses. You ask her what this is for, and she says, "For the refugees." What refugees? You know that Jane's mother suffered from mental illness, and you worry that something like that might be troubling Jane, so you asked her to see a psychiatrist. The psychiatrist doesn't find anything in the realm of mental illness, so you stop worrying about her storing things in the barn. There has been an uprising in Hungary. Maybe those are the refugees Jane is preparing for.

In his new position with Dell Paperbacks, Knox Burger, knowing your need for cash, suggests that you write a science fiction novel for his new line of mass-market paperback originals. You put together an outline for the book right away. Unlike your other novels, the writing of this one comes easily. You are familiar with science fiction and especially admire the work of writers like Isaac Asimov and Theodore Sturgeon, but if you become known for that genre in your era, you will be put in a drawer of writers who won't be taken seriously by the literary critics (you note decades later that the days of "genreism" have happily faded). Regardless, you sail through the writing and call the book *The Sirens of Titan*.

In 1958, you learn that your beloved sister, Allie, at age forty-one, is dying of cancer. Allie is the person in your family you've always been closest to. You believe that to write well, whether you are writing a story, novel, or play, you should write with a particular person in mind, the person you imagine you are writing to. You believe that you can't just sit down and write something as if it's addressed "to the world" and have it turn out well. Allie is the person you've always imagined you are writing to and for.

Allie is in the hospital in Newark, New Jersey, dying of cancer. Her husband, Jim Adams, is on a commuter train from New Jersey to his job in New York City. The train crosses a river and the bridge collapses, plunging all the passengers into the river and to their deaths. Someone brings a newspaper with that story to Allie. The next day, she dies of cancer at age forty-one. You and Jane realize her four sons, ages fourteen, eleven, nine, and twenty-one months, have suddenly become orphans.

Without any thought as to finances or the logistics of adding four children to your own family of three children, you go at once to New Jersey and bring the Adams boys and their two dogs and rabbit back to Barnstable. It's a good thing you bought that big house!

It's a good thing the house has a barn and a good thing that Jane has been gathering old blankets and clothing and storing them there. You and your children wondered why she was doing that and who "the refugees" were that she said she was saving them for. Well, now you know. It turns out your sister's boys are "the refugees." They are lovingly integrated into the family except for the smallest son, a baby whom relatives of Allie's husband, Jim, insist on raising themselves in Birmingham, Alabama. You and Jane now have six children (plus the dogs and the rabbit). Your financial situation is still more precarious, but you manage to keep everyone in food and clothing.

Within the family, the Adams boys are referred to as "The Orphans," which becomes, in your family, a loving label. To make them feel completely a part of the family, as much a part of the family as your own children, you suggest they continue to call you and Jane "Aunt Jane" and "Uncle Kurt," and your own children start addressing you by the same titles, so instead of "Mother" and "Father," you are "Aunt Jane" and "Uncle Kurt." Since Nanny, your youngest child, called you and Jane "Mother" and "Father," she now calls you "Aunt Mother" and "Uncle Father."

Mark says later, "I had a lot of hope, and in the end I was right, that good things would come of having our cousins come live with us . . . The cousins were a breath of fresh air. I was glad for the company."

We wish you a Happy New Year!

* A D A M S *

V O N N E G U T *

Nan Peter Steve Jim Edie Mark Tiger

It is often reported that you and Jane adopted these boys, but in fact, you did not legally adopt them, because legal fees would have been way beyond your budget. You and Jane simply raise them as if they are your own, and your children treat their cousins as brothers. Sometimes in interviews you simply say they were adopted, as it is a comfortable kind of shorthand that is easier to explain to people.

* * *

On April 15, 1959, you write to the publisher of *Player Piano*, Charles Scribner's Sons. The novel you refer to as "Cat's Call" will be titled *Cat's Cradle*.

Gentlemen,

You have been in possession of a portion of a novel of mine, "Cat's Call," for more than two years now. This surely constitutes a rejection. Would you kindly return the manuscript to me at the earliest possible convenience.

I realize that you are in the position of trying to protect an investment of several hundred dollars. However, the best chance for you to recover that money, it seems to me, is to let me submit the novel elsewhere. You would share in the advance, if any. I think I could talk a paperback house into an advance that would make us both happy.

You write to Knox Burger in the summer of 1959: "As for *The Sirens of Titan:* I have made all the revisions suggested by Jane, and this morning, the messy manuscript goes to a typist. In ten days, she promises a flawless original and one carbon. I will send the original to you and the carbon to Ken and Max [Littauer and Wilkinson]. And that will be that, I think. You must know how grateful I am for your having given me the chance to do the book and for your having showed it around to hard-cover people, and for all the rest of it."

Knox has left Dell to move to Fawcett Gold Medal Books, another paperback house, but *Sirens* is still published by Dell, with a first printing of 175,000 paperback copies. It gains a popular audience but gets no reviews.

You write to Knox again that summer: you had wanted to get the Guggenheim Fellowship so you could go to

Germany and visit Dresden to, you hoped, bring back memories of your experience there for the book you still hope to write about it.

> The Guggenheims turned me down. . . . And tell me—when one is being frog-marched by life, does one giggle or does one try to maintain as much dignity as possible under the circumstances?
>
> I got an extremely friendly letter back from Ray Bradbury [the most prominent science fiction writer of the era]. I called him Mr. Bradbury and he called me Kurt. I told him I was thinking of moving to California, and he said sure, come ahead. He said he would introduce me to some people, and he said it was warm all the time out there. Can you imagine someplace where it's warm all the time?

When things are tough, you imagine going to California, but you don't go. Moving to California is a historic syndrome in the lives of American writers, ever since F. Scott Fitzgerald's end-of-life years there became a legend. (I fell victim to it in midlife; you never did).

9.

FINALLY LANDING

The sixties in America was destined to be a turbulent decade. After the "togetherness" of World War II and its aftermath of peace and prosperity, most white Americans and even Europeans seemed to love America—until the war in Vietnam tore the fabric of the nation and divided it into hostile camps. For black Americans, the fabric of the nation was already being torn by the riots in the ghettos of American cities as James Baldwin predicted in *The Fire Next Time*. In the chaos that follows, three American leaders are assassinated—Martin Luther King, Jr., Bobby Kennedy, and Malcolm X. President Lyndon B. Johnson announces he will not seek reelection as protestors chant, "LBJ, LBJ, how many kids did you kill today?"

As Mark Vonnegut writes in his spellbinding memoir *Just Like Someone Without Mental Illness Only More So*, "Our parents and teachers were demoralized by the war and how imperfect America, the world's last best hope, was turning out. After the Ohio National Guard loaded up with live ammunition and killed four students at Kent State, no one knew what to expect or where things were going."

The long-haired, bearded beatniks of the fifties become the hippies who read Jack Kerouac's *On the Road* and spread out to all parts of the national youth culture. They are led in chants for peace by Kerouac's poet pal Allen Ginsberg, whose "Human Be-In" I attend with hundreds of others in a San Francisco park in the summer of 1967 ("the Summer of Love"). "Flower power" is hopefully posed against napalm power as Ginsberg leads us in chanting, "Ohmmmmmm . . ."

Young people discover your books—*Cat's Cradle* is the catalyst. The book is a stew of provocative ideas, including a made-up religion called "Bokononism." The main plot involves a character named Professor Hoenikker who worked on the atomic bomb and accidentally discovers a new way of ending the world—this time with *"ice-nine,"* a crystal that turns all water solid, including the oceans of the world.

You began this book in the 1950s, a decade that was obsessed with the fear that, since we had dropped atomic bombs on Hiroshima and Nagasaki to end World War II, our main opponent in the Cold War, the Soviet Union, had developed its own atomic bomb—and other countries were developing their own too, with the potential for a worldwide conflagration. Americans built bomb shelters in backyards, and debates were held about the morality of whom to allow into your bomb shelter in case of an attack—relatives, neighbors, friends? "Air raid drills" were held in public schools, and children hunched under desks that supposedly would save them from atomic attack and radiation.

With a mix of satire and seriousness, you tackle the big issues in *Cat's Cradle*—issues like the possible end of the world. You got your idea for the creation of a substance like *ice-nine* when you spoke to that physicist at a party your brother Bernie threw when you both were at GE. Nothing is lost on you. You find a way to use in your fiction whatever you learn, in classes in anthropology, in working as a reporter at the City News Bureau of Chicago, and from your days as a public relations man for GE. Seemingly overnight, you start being called "a spokesman of the young generation," to which you reply that you are not a spokesman for anyone or anything.

It's ironic that you are labeled a hero of "the counterculture" when you are so out of tune with its styles, substances, and its Eastern spiritual practices. From Iowa, you write to Knox that Jane has taken up "transcendental meditation." Her guru is Maharishi Mahesh Yogi, whom you go to hear speak in Cambridge, Massachusetts, and skewer in a piece for *Esquire* called "Yes, We Have No Nirvanas."

You put down the idea that the higher wisdom is to be found in Eastern religions and their meditative practices. You say that we in the West have our own practice that quiets the mind, lowers the pulse rate, and brings a sense of relaxation. It is called "reading short stories." You say that reading a short story is like a "Buddhist catnap." You smoke a joint with Jerry Garcia, leader of the iconic band the Grateful Dead, but it doesn't do much for you. You stick to your bourbon and Pall Malls and reading short stories to relax.

✳✳✳

In Knox's new job, he signs you up to write a book about an American living in Germany who becomes a "double agent," broadcasting propaganda for the Nazis and giving secret information to the Americans. The working title of the book is *Nation of Two*. It will become the novel *Mother Night*. You write to Knox in January of 1960, "Most people aren't very good at their jobs. You are superlative at yours, which is editing, and, since I am a writer, my gratitude is extravagant."

Money is always a problem, especially since you now are supporting a household of six children—three of your own and three of your sister's.

Jane says, "What we are mainly living on is hope."

Mark later says, "My mother always believed more than my father did that he would someday be a famous writer and it would all be worth it."

You borrow $300 from the money Mark has saved from his paper route.

Despite such desperate measures, all is not gloom and doom in the realm of Vonnegut. Mark remembers one night when you and Jane go out to pick up a broom and some lightbulbs, and while you are in the department store, there is music playing. You notice it's a waltz, and you turn to Jane and ask her to dance. The two of you waltz down an aisle, and the music changes to a fox-trot. You switch to that step, and the two of you fox-trot up another aisle. The music keeps changing—fast, slow, rumba, tango. Whatever music is thrown at you, the two of you respond with the appropriate step. After fifteen minutes or so of trying to stump you, whoever is watching you through the shoplifting-surveillance system gives up, and the public-address system goes silent. You and Jane come home laughing so hard you are crying.

* * *

The ups and downs of your fortune make you feel as if you're riding a roller coaster, one of those steep and scary ones. You sometimes talk casually about the possibility of committing suicide. Like your mother did.

Sometimes you play chess with Mark, who takes up the game as naturally as if he were born with the moves in his genes. Sometimes when you see that he has you trapped and there's no escape, you pick up the chessboard and hurl it across the room, kings and queens and bishops flying.

Your daughters duck. They urge Mark to let you win, but the problem is you're good enough to know that's what he's doing, and you don't allow it.

***

Because you have been turned down for the job teaching English at Cape Cod Community College, you take a new job at a school for boys with behavior problems. Not only is the paycheck important, but you write to Knox in July of 1961, "I am glad you find life stimulating. I do, too, kind of—but not nearly enough. I am hoping this teaching job will fill me with a little more zowie."

To provide you some zowie as well as some more cash, Knox collects a selection of a dozen short stories from the three dozen you have published since 1950 in the "slick" magazines along with some sci-fi pulp magazines and publishes them in a Fawcett Gold Medal paperback called *Canary in a Cathouse.*

Mother Night, your novel about the German American double agent, is also published in 1961. The main character is an American who is raised in Germany from age eleven. As a man, he becomes a radio propagandist for the Nazis in World War II. In real life, there were no German Americans who became Nazi propagandists—the English-speaking Nazi propagandist known as Lord Haw-Haw was in fact an Englishman.

A "lesson" from that novel becomes a piece of wise advice to many of your appreciative readers: be careful what you pretend to be, for you may become what you pretend to be.

You write to Knox in spring 1963, "The thing I did for Dell [*Cat's Cradle*] took me ten years to do, although it wasn't worth anything like ten years—and I have a sense of an era's having ended. I never used to wonder what to do next. Now I wonder what in hell to do next."

In January of 1963, you write to Knox referring to the teaching job at the school for boys with behavioral problems, "I quit the teaching job, after doggedly finishing out a full semester. It was killing work, and I don't mind work all that much but it was a racket, too. I'll tell you how the racket works some time. I'm writing a play about it."

That was another source of income that is now snuffed out, and it is little wonder that you fantasize about a multimillionaire who decides to give away all his money to the poor. Of course, he is thought to be insane. God bless him, though. You work hard to write his story as your next novel, *God Bless You, Mr. Rosewater*. Writing this novel gives you another opportunity to point out the inequality of wealth in this country. You write of the people who live near "the money river" and those who live far away from it.

April 9, 1964

Dear old Knox:

   Hey listen—I have just finished a book about twenty minutes ago, and do I ever feel loony and great. Happy as a bird. Tweet, tweet, tweet. . . .

   Boy am I happy.

There is money coming in.

The novel, titled *God Bless You, Mr. Rosewater, or Pearls Before Swine,* will be published in the following spring in hardcover by Holt, Rinehart and Winston and will be the first of your books to be widely reviewed.

***

You take Nanny and her best friend to the New York World's Fair, and you stop on the way to pay a visit to dear Bernard O'Hare, your old war buddy. You and Bernard are sitting around in his kitchen trying to evoke memories of the Dresden experience. During your talk, Bernard's wife, Mary, keeps coming into the kitchen where you are talking. She is obviously not pleased. She's banging pots and pans around and slamming doors. You wonder why she is so mad at you. You and Bernard come up with a few stray memories, which don't amount to much.

   Mary is still making noise. She takes a tray of ice cubes

from the freezer and bangs it in the sink even though there is plenty of ice out. Then she turns to you, lets you see how angry she is and that the anger is for you. She has been talking to herself, so what she says is a fragment of a much larger conversation. "You were just babies in the war—like the ones upstairs!" she says.

You nod. "It's true. We were foolish virgins in the war, right at the end of childhood."

"But you're not going to write it that way, are you." Mary says.

This isn't a question; it's an accusation.

"I don't know," you say.

"Well, *I* know," she says. "You'll pretend you were men instead of babies, and you'll be played in the movies by Frank Sinatra and John Wayne or some of those other glamorous, war-loving, dirty old men. And war will look just wonderful, so we'll have a lot more of them. And they'll be fought by babies like the babies upstairs."

So now you understand. It's war that made her so angry. She doesn't want her babies or anybody else's babies killed in wars. And she thinks wars are partly inspired by books and movies.

You hold up your right hand, and you make her a promise.

"Mary," you say, "I don't think this book of mine is ever going to be finished. I must have written five thousand pages by now, and thrown them all away. If I ever do finish it, though, I give you my word of honor: there won't be a part for Frank Sinatra or John Wayne."

***

It's as if this talk with Mary O'Hare breaks the logjam, the long struggle that has blocked the book that's inside you. You no longer have to worry about battles and strategies, conquests and defeats, heroes and enemies. You only need to tell your story. Your imagination is free, and you can soar into different times and places, from Ilium, New York, to the planet Tralfamadore, from 1945 to 1965 and beyond and before. Your imagination is no longer stuck in the petrified forest of old war novels, so Billy Pilgrim can become "unstuck in time."

You finish the book and call it *Slaughterhouse-Five, or The Children's Crusade*. Of course you dedicate it to Mary O'Hare, as well as to Gerhard Müller, the taxi driver who took you and Bernard O'Hare around Dresden and who hoped the three of you would meet again "If the accident will." You had that talk with Mary O'Hare, and in terms of being able to write the book, the accident did.

***

God Bless You, Mr. Rosewater is respectfully reviewed. The *Washington Post* says, "Vonnegut's new novel confirms his unique and outrageous talent." The *New York Times* offers an unconventional review to suit an unconventional narrative: "Here is a book that is devoid of anything as square as a plot, its text broken up into short epiphanies, like poetic cantos. . . . This is a writer with an excellent ear, a knack for arresting imagery, and a Message."

Many of the reviews of *Rosewater* acknowledge the other books you have written—*Player Piano*, *The Sirens of Titan*, and *Mother Night*. Recognition by prestigious publications puts you on the literary map. This development brings you to the attention of the Iowa Writers' Workshop and its faculty and administration. They had asked the poet Robert Lowell to come teach there in the fall of 1965, but at the last minute, he was unable to do it. You are invited to fill his spot. You write to John Gerber, chairman of the English Department of the University of Iowa, on July 11, 1965:

> Dear Dr. Gerber:
> I'm very pleased to be invited out there. What writer wouldn't be? . . . My wife and children will stay here. There are too many of them to move.

To Knox on August 7, 1965, you write:

> I suppose I'll take off for Iowa City about September 10. I don't want to go, but everybody says it will be good for me. Jane will be left here with just two little girls. Think of it, all the people who used to live here. It will be a strangely good winter for Jane.

Finally Landing

149

She has taken up the piano, and, with me gone, she'll take up reading and writing again. She used to be excellent at both. . . .

Did I understand you correctly—that you are thinking of becoming an agent?

Yes, Knox is going to become an agent. He assumes that you will be his first client.

***

Iowa turns out to be just what you need. You find there the "zowie" you had hoped for when you taught at the school for boys with behavioral problems. This is not only "a teaching job" or "teaching at Iowa." This is the Iowa Writers' Workshop, one of the first two graduate writing programs in the United States along with Stanford's. It is hard to realize today, with the graduate writing programs established all across the country, that before 1936, there were no advanced degrees offered in creative writing by any American universities. When I graduated from Columbia College in 1955, I had never heard of any graduate writing program among my many aspiring writer friends or even by my professors. Mark Van Doren, the Pulitzer Prize–winning poet who had helped establish the required literature program of Columbia's core curriculum, told students it was more important to read than to write during the college years; absorbing the great books, he said, was the best instruction for writing.

In the sixties, the Iowa Writers' Workshop features established writers coming to teach for one or two semesters as well as two writers on permanent staff, so students are exposed to different styles, ideas, and approaches to writing.

In the time you teach there, writers on the staff include Nelson Algren, famous at the time for his novel *The Man with the Golden Arm*, which became a hit movie starring Frank Sinatra, as well as Vance Bourjaily, known for his first novel, *The End of My Life*, and the Chilean novelist José Donoso. In your second year at Iowa, the novelist Richard Yates arrives, and he becomes a good friend for life. Except for the World War II novelist Norman Mailer, who came to live on the Cape every summer and dropped in for a couple of visits, you never knew any other working writers during your years in Barnstable. Your neighbors didn't seem to know or care what you did for a living, while your Indianapolis relatives expressed their displeasure.

Your uncle John Rauch, a Harvard graduate and Indianapolis lawyer, wrote you a postcard in response to your novel *Cat's Cradle*: "You're saying that life is a load of crap, right? Read Thackery!" You dedicated *The Sirens of Titan* to Uncle Alex, and he told you he couldn't read it but he supposed young people liked it.

Before classes begin at Iowa, you and the others on the faculty appear before the students to tell them something about yourself and your ideas about writing and what they might expect in your course. You are wielding a long black cigarette holder, and the students are curious and intrigued. One of them, Suzanne McConnell, says you "struck [her] funny bone."

On September 28, 1965, you write to Jane:

> Dearest Jane . . .
>
> My enormous Form of Fiction class, which has grown to about 80 students, and which is still growing, thanks to late registrants, is being broken up into two sections ("A" and "B"—what else?), each meeting for two hours once a week. . . .
>
> I have incidentally changed the name of my course, since I am the only one teaching it, to Form and *Texture* of Fiction. Hi ho. It's going pretty well. At our first meeting, the students were bitter about the hugeness of the class. They're somewhat mollified by its being divided up, and I'm starting to get some friendly playback. They're starting to catch on that Mr. Vonnegut can be funny. That's the only thing I know how to be, and of course never got the chance to be funny in Barnstable. You've got to take the goods with the bads.
>
> Anyway, as you can see: when you come out here for your first visit, we can go to Chicago (six hours by car), or do anything else we damn please after class on Wednesday. If you are as interested in sex as you say you are, there is a really lovely book about it in my study—on the top shelf. It's red, and it's called *The ABZ of Love.*
>
> Love from A to Z—
>
> K

You write to your daughter Nanny on September 30, 1965, to report: "I am getting a lot of good work done here, which is why I came here. I write a lot, and teach a lot. The students say they like me, and they have gone out and bought books I have written, and they say they like those, too."

You invite your daughter Edie to come out and stay with you while she continues high school. She finds the University High School in Iowa City "a paradise." Jane comes out in November but has to go back to nurse her dotty mother, who is recovering from a broken hip in your house on the Cape.

In January 1966, you write to Knox:

> Speaking of wives—good old Jane will be here in a week or two with Nanny, will stay till summer. Something telepathic has busted between us, and I don't know how to fix it. I'd like to fix it. Sometimes when I talk to her I feel like the Ambassador from New Zealand presenting his credentials to the Foreign Minister of Uruguay. It's formal and strange, and not at all sexy. . . . She's a darling, loyal girl. . . . I dunno. We'll fix it up some way.
>
> At Christmas I had the damnedest revulsion to Cape Cod, loved my family but hated the house—I don't want to live there any more.

You are enjoying being among well-known writers for the first time. Sometimes, you confess, you feel a little awkward when you talk to Nelson Algren, who's the most famous one there. You sign one of your own books to him saying he is one of the few important artists of your time, and he is the only one you know.

On April 3, 1966, you write to Knox: "I don't feel much like writing any more, and I don't feel sad about it, either. Within the next few months I'll finish the Dresden book, which will be about the size of the Bobbsey Twins, and that'll be the end for a while. It reads like a telegram, and it's the one I always thought it was my duty to write."

You write to Knox again on October 28, 1966: "The Guggenheim Foundation wrote, saying that I had been mentioned to them as a guy who might make a good Guggenheimer. So I applied."

You submit your Dresden novel, *Slaughterhouse-Five*, to Holt, Rinehart and Winston, who published *Cat's Cradle* in hardcover. They turn it down.

You remember a fan letter from the publisher Seymour Lawrence, who enjoyed the review you wrote in the *New York Times* of a new Random House dictionary. Lawrence was the editor of the Atlantic Monthly Press when he was twenty eight years old. He started his own imprint in a one-room office on Beacon Street in Boston in 1965 in partnership with Delacorte/Dell in New York. He told you that if you were ever in need of a publisher, you should knock on his door at 90 Beacon Street.

Over Christmas vacation of 1966, you're home on the Cape, and from there you go into Boston to knock on the door of Mr. Lawrence. Your Dresden novel, *Slaughterhouse-Five*, has also now been turned down by the two other publishers who have brought out books of yours in hardcover editions. You tell Lawrence about the rejections and ask if he is interested in reading it. He reads it quickly and calls you into his office to offer you the best deal you've ever had. Since Lawrence is publishing his line of books through Delacorte, which is part of the same company as Dell Paperbacks, he is able to offer authors a contract for both hardcover and paperback rights. This is revolutionary at the time.

Lawrence not only wants to publish *Slaughterhouse-Five*, but he also feels your work is powerfully in tune with the times, and he offers you a contract for *Slaughterhouse-Five* and two more of your books with an advance of $35,000 for hardcover and paperback rights to each book.

"You shouldn't give me that much money," you say.

"Why not?" Lawrence asks.

"Because my books don't make money," you tell him.

Lawrence says, "You write the books, and I'll worry about the money."

Neither you nor Sam Lawrence will ever have to worry about money again.

You write to Lawrence on February 4, 1967:

Dear Sam:

I'm glad you're glad. I can't imagine that you are as happy as I am. You're putting me on my feet as a writer. I've been living off-balance ever since I started freelancing in 1950. We'll do some good books together.

Robie Macauley, fiction editor of *Playboy* magazine, buys your story "Welcome to the Monkey House." This will be in a new collection using the short stories from your earlier collection, *Canary in a Cat House*, but published as a hardcover book with the new story as the title of the book, *Welcome to the Monkey House*, to be published by Delacorte Press/Seymour Lawrence.

Robert Scholes, the literary critic and English professor, whom you get to know at Iowa, includes you in a new book of literary criticism called *The Fabulators*, which discusses the work of well-known, innovative writers. It's the first recognition and praise that you receive from a prominent literary critic.

Scholes writes, "Vonnegut, in his fiction, is doing what the most serious writers always do. He is helping, in Joyce's phrase, 'to create the conscience of the race.' What race? Human, certainly. Not American or German or any other abstraction from humanity. Just as pure romance provides us with necessary psychic exercise, intellectual comedy like Vonnegut's offers us moral stimulation—not fixed ethical positions, which we can complacently assume, but such thoughts as exercise our consciences and help us keep our humanity in shape, ready to respond to the humanity of others."

Your application for a Guggenheim Fellowship was turned down in 1959; now, in 1967, you are awarded a Guggenheim in 1967 to go to Dresden and do more research for *Slaughterhouse-Five*. Sam Lawrence was happy with the draft you showed him, but you felt that there was still work to be done.

Many young men are becoming pacifists or doing whatever they can to evade the draft. This is not primarily because they are against war on principle but because they are against *this* war, the war in Vietnam. In March of 1966, a group of young men gathered at a rally on the Boston Common and burned their draft cards. Other young men flee to Canada to avoid the draft, establishing an American community of young people in Toronto. The former Harvard professor and psychedelic experimenter and advocate Timothy Leary becomes a guru to young people, who adopt his slogan "Turn on, tune in, drop out."

On November 28, you write to the draft board in Hyannis, Massachusetts, asking that Mark be exempt from the draft:

> Gentlemen:
>   My son Mark Vonnegut is registered with you. He is now in the process of requesting classification as a conscientious objector. I thoroughly approve of what he is doing. It is in keeping with the way I have raised him. All his life he has learned hatred for killing from me.

I was a volunteer in the Second World War. I was an infantry scout, saw plenty of action, was finally captured and served about six months as a prisoner of war in Germany. I have a Purple Heart. I was honorably discharged. I am entitled, it seems to me, to pass on to my son my opinion of killing. I don't even hunt or fish anymore. I have some guns which I inherited, but they are covered with rust.

This attitude toward killing is a matter between my God and me. I do not participate much in organized religion. I have read the Bible a lot. I preach, after a fashion. I write books which express my disgust for people who find it easy and reasonable to kill.

We say grace at meals, taking turns. Every member of my large family has been called upon often to thank God for blessings which have been ours. What Mark is doing now is in the service of God, Whose Son was exceedingly un-warlike.

There isn't a grain of cowardice in this. Mark is a strong, courageous young man. What he is doing requires more guts than I ever had—and more decency.

My family has been in this country for five generations now. My ancestors came here to escape the militaristic madness and tyranny of Europe, and to gain the freedom to answer the dictates of their own consciences. They and their descendants have been good citizens and proud to be Americans. Mark is proud to be an American, and, in his father's opinion, he is being an absolutely first-rate citizen now.

He will not hate.

He will not kill.

There's hope in that. There's no hope in war.

Yours truly,

Kurt Vonnegut, Jr.

On April 22, 1968, you write to Robert Scholes: "I am about a week from finishing the new novel. It sure has been hard. It isn't very long. From now on I am going to follow familiar models and make a lot of dough."

You are never going to follow familiar models, but you do make a lot of dough.

***

That spring you speak at a literary conference at the University of Notre Dame. One of the other speakers is Joseph Heller, a World War II veteran of the air force and author of the satiric World War II novel *Catch-22*. This begins a lifelong friendship. Several years later you and Heller are guests of honor at a literary event in Fort Lauderdale, Florida, where authors are invited to dinners at the homes of wealthy sponsors of the festival. As you and Heller walk into the living room of a large and lavish home with paintings by famous artists on the walls that are worth millions, you ask him if it makes him feel bad that any one of these paintings is worth more money than all of his profits from *Catch-22*.

"No," Heller says, "because I have something this man will never have."

"What's that?"

"I know when I have enough," Heller says.

* * *

You write to Mark on May 28, 1968:

> Dear Mark:
>
> I ask a favor for your mother's sake: please look awfully nice at your graduation. She is a dear, romantic girl, and I want her to be as happy as she can possibly be at the graduation of her only son.
>
> I am talking about hair, of course. The beard is fine, and characteristic and, hence, beloved by one and all. What I am suggesting is that the hair on top of your head be styled somewhat—that you look like nobody else on this earth, perhaps, but, in a movie star way, look handsome as hell all the same. So she'll nearly swoon. You have achieved this before. You can achieve it again.
>
> Edith promises to be home in time for your graduation. Promises, promises.
>
> Love,
>
> K

After Mark graduates from Swarthmore, he and his

friends start a commune in British Columbia. Communes of idealistic young people are being formed around the country, particularly in New England and on the West Coast.

***

On July 18, 1968, Sam Lawrence publishes *Welcome to the Monkey House.* You dedicate the book:

> For Knox Burger
> Ten days older than I am.
> He has been a very good
> father to me.

> Dear Knox:
>   I am glad that my dedication tickled you. I thought you would be jaded by now. How many books have been dedicated to you so far? Twenty, I'll bet. . . .
>   About smoking: it takes two weeks to quit. Unless you have two free weeks, forget it. Expect to act crazy. I sure did.
>   Cheers,
>   Kurt

A friend in New York City gets an advance copy of the *New York Times Book Review* and calls you to read Robert Scholes's front-page review of *Slaughterhouse-Five.* Scholes proclaims you "a true artist" who is "among the best writers of his generation."

You send a telegram to Scholes on April 4, 1969, after hearing his review:

> spy in new york read *times* review to me on telephone.
> WOW. next time your kid comes for HANDOUT, he gets caviar and hummingbird'S tongues. love
> croesus

Your son, Mark, reports that you "went from being poor to being famous and rich in the blink of an eye."

Slaughterhouse-Five is a national best seller, and eager fans line up for your autograph at bookstores throughout the country—except at the bookstore of L. S. Ayres, a leading department store in your hometown of Indianapolis, which you report to me, your fellow Hoosier, on May 9, 1969.:

> Dear Dan,
>
> At the request of Ayres, I went to Indianapolis last week, appeared on a TV and a radio show, then signed books in the bookstore. I sold thirteen books in two hours, every one of them to a relative. Word of honor.
>
> The next book is about Indianapolis. Yours, too, I bet. I stopped by Shortridge, which is still unbelievably great.
>
> Peace,
> Kurt

In fact, my new book *is* about Indianapolis, and when I finish writing it in August of 1969, my agent sends it to ten publishers. Only three are interested, and only one really loves the book. The one who loves it is Seymour Lawrence, who has just had his biggest hit with *Slaughterhouse-Five*. (Maybe he thinks writers from Indianapolis are good luck).

He has to get the support of his partners at Delacorte, who might worry that a first novel by a writer who has published only journalistic books is a bad risk. Lawrence calls me and asks if he can send my book to you to see if you'll give it a plug.

"I'm not sure it's a good idea," I say. "I've only met the man once in my life, and my novel isn't at all like his own work."

I don't mention that our bond is not about literature but about failure at high school sports.

Lawrence says a quote from you could make all the difference, so, not very hopefully, I say OK. Three days later, Lawrence calls to read me a telegram you sent him about my novel: "you must publish this important book. get this boy in our stable."

I knew we'd be friends for life.

* * *

You write to Sam Lawrence on October 17, 1969:

> This is to tell you that you had better cancel all plans for the
> new book, *Breakfast of Champions.* I've stopped work on it
> for reasons of health.
>
> I've got to quit smoking. When I do that, I quit writing.
> So there we are. I know. I've been through it before.
>
> Sorry—but I don't want to suffocate.

10.

GOODBYE AND GOODBYE
AND GOODBYE

You and Jane come up to Boston in the spring to take me to dinner to celebrate the coming publication of my novel, which will come out in July. I feel like I should take *you* to dinner for all you have done for my book. You and Jane seem as cheerful as ever. Why shouldn't you be? It seems as if Jane's faith in you has been fulfilled, and it was all worth it. I suspect no big change in your life when you come to Boston to meet with Lawrence later that spring and take me to lunch at Jake Wirth's, a German restaurant with sawdust on the floor.

You and I and Sam Lawrence (he is now "our publisher") are invited to visit a commune in Vermont started by some young writers and their friends from Boston. They appoint us "honorary uncles" of the commune, which they call Total Loss Farm, and escort us on a grand tour of the place. You are especially interested, since your son, Mark, is still living on the commune in British Columbia.

Ray Mungo, the untitled leader of the commune, is a

bright and talented young writer who was editor of the *BU News* when he was at Boston University. Ray shows us around the place, explaining the hopes of the people living there. He is very proud of the vegetable garden, hoping it will help make the place self-sustaining.

"We want to be the last people on earth," he says.

Sam Lawrence and I nod, impressed by the notion, but you have a question: "Isn't that kind of a stuck-up thing to want to be?"

Everyone laughs, including Ray. I have not heard the term "stuck-up" since high school, but it seems just right, blowing the grandiosity out of the balloon. It's the kind of "impolite," unexpected term that pops up in your writing.

You go to New York in September to watch rehearsals of your play *Happy Birthday, Wanda June*, based on your first play, *Penelope*, originally performed on Cape Cod nearly twenty years earlier.

As you write in the introduction to the book publication of the play, "It was a time of change, of goodbyes and goodbyes and goodbyes."

You leave the people and places that have supported you for your whole "writing life" since you left your job at GE. You leave your wife and your marriage of twenty-five years and the editor who published your first stories and three of your novels, who has now become a literary agent, and you leave the landscape of Barnstable Harbor to buy a house smack in the middle of Manhattan.

Seismic cracks had already appeared in your marriage, as you reported in letters to Knox when you were teaching at Iowa, in which you also talked about your feelings of alienation from the Barnstable house when you went back for Christmas vacation from Iowa City. You say, "I was drinking more and arguing a lot and I had to get out of that house."

You write to Knox on September 11, 1970:

> Dear Knox—
>
> I'm sad and embarrassed about what business consider-ations and other muggy matters have done to our friendship. You're right—there *is* a lack of comfortableness there. As for your backing off: continue to name me as a client, if that is at all useful. I'll continue to recommend you to others gladly, and to say you are one of two agents I have—if that is at all useful. The reality is that Max [your longtime agent, Max Wilkinson] is so deeply woven into my past that he has sold or is entitled to sell virtually everything I'll write for the next dozen years. Also: I am going more deeply into the theater business with partners—and lawyers will necessarily do most of my negotiating from now on.
>
> Yours truly,
>
> Kurt

* * *

You form what will become a lifelong professional alliance with the theatrical attorney Don Farber, whom you met at a dinner party in Long Island. Farber now serves as your agent, negotiator, and advisor in personal as well as professional matters. Don and his wife, Annie, become close friends of yours.

You borrow "a tiny penthouse" from a friend near the Theatre De Lys in Greenwich Village to use when you come down and watch rehearsals of your play. The play opens October 7 to mixed reviews, from *Newsweek*'s "Vonnegut's dialogue is not only fast and funny, with a palpable taste and crackle, but it also means something" to the *New Republic*'s "a disaster, full of callow wit, romantic rheumatic invention, and dormitory profundity." After the play opens, you rent a one-bedroom apartment on East Fifty-First Street, commuting two days a week to teach a writing class at Harvard. You never return to live in the house on Cape Cod.

On one of your teaching days in Cambridge, you invite me to have lunch in Harvard Square. You introduce me to Jill Krementz, who joins us for lunch. She's a photographer who has come to "chronicle" your teaching the Harvard writing class. She is pleasant and friendly. I don't realize then she will become more than a "chronicler."

Despite the mixed reviews of *Wanda June*, it revives your old dream that dates back to the original production of *Penelope* on Cape Cod. You write to your friend José Donoso on December 2, 1970, that despite your report that "The adventure of having a play produced was harrowing" and your own assessment that the play was "clumsy and sophomoric," you still harbor the hope of becoming a full-time playwright. You tell Donoso that "I had to begin my theatrical career with something—and now I have in fact begun. I've written six novels. Now I want to write six plays."

You are one of the most successful novelists in America, and you have written only one original full-length play that's ever been produced, and you keep rewriting it. And yet you would rather be a playwright than a novelist!

You once told Sam Lawrence, "You are programmed to be a publisher, and I was programmed to be a writer." In spite of your playwriting dreams, it is obvious you are "programmed to be a novelist," not a playwright. You write another eight novels but no other plays. (You can't keep giving *Penelope* another name and trying to get it produced again).

You write to Knox on December 30: "Strange year just ending. Wish I knew where I was—or maybe that's exactly what I don't want to find out."

* * *

One night when you are sitting alone in that apartment and drinking some bourbon, you think about high school and the football coach who gave you the "Charles Atlas

Bodybuilding Course" in front of the other students. You call information in Indianapolis and get the phone number of the coach. It is late, but you don't care if you wake him up. When he answers the phone, you say, "This is Kurt Vonnegut. You probably don't remember me. I wanted to tell you my body turned out just fine."

***

On February 26, you write to Sam Lawrence:

> It is true that I have started working on *Breakfast of Champions* again, slowly and painfully, from the very beginning. It takes me so long to find out what my books are about, so I can write them. If I had pressed onward with the book before, and finished it willy nilly, it would have been an enormous fake. It probably would have made us a fortune. . . . Come see me soon. . . . I've stopped horsing around so much. I have now met George Plimpton [publisher of the *Paris Review* and noted host of literary parties] so I've reached the peak of my career as a social butterfly. Back to work.
> Cheers,
> Kurt Vonnegut Jr.

You try to make a transition with Jane to "the new abnormal." You write to her on March 7, 1971:

Dear Jane—

. . . We hurt each other back and forth so much, almost absent-mindedly, that it was common sense for us to separate, if only to break the rhythm. And it has accidentally been good for Edie, having me here. I went with her to a literary bash thrown by George Plimpton last night, at a restaurant called Elaine's. She was the most attractive woman there. Larry Rivers, the painter, spent his whole time with her. She was like Liza Doolittle at the ball. Everybody wanted to know who she was. She is so cool through it all. She is very at home in the world.

Any word from Mark? None here.

Margaret Meade says that any couple which has had children has an irreversible and undissolvable relationship, which is what you say obliquely in your good letter today. I agree. It is deep and permanent.

I will have to come up there in the next couple of weeks to put the finishing touches on the mother-fucking income taxes. Amazing amounts of cash will wing their way from us to the Pentagon. Too bad. . . .

K

***

You write to José Donoso on March 23, 1971:

Dear Pepe:

My son, Mark, has had a nervous breakdown, and has

been diagnosed as schizophrenic. He is in a hospital in British Columbia. I have visited him. Jane is out there now.

* * *

On June 1, 1971, you write to Nanny.

Dear old Nanny—

You certainly deserve a letter from me. A hundred letters would be more like it, I love you so.

I will be home from time to time to see you. But I will not stay for long. I still love your mother, but we can't be together much without fighting. We have tried to do things about this, but nothing helps, and each fight hurts more than the last one.

I wasn't stolen away by another woman. I don't think people can steal other people. I simply went away because the fighting was making everybody so unhappy. I've done that several times before. Going to Iowa was an example. Every time I went away I simply went to aloneness. There was never any other woman beckoning me to come.

This time, for instance, I couldn't make myself come home after the play opened, and I was alone. I hardly knew Jill at all, and I didn't like her much, and whatever between us happened long after I decided home was too uncomfortable for me.

And, as you know perfectly well, people need people. And Jill is who I have now. She's awfully nice to me. I was the one who sent you the picture of you and me in Greenwich Village. I wanted you to have it.

I don't know what will happen next. I'll keep in touch. I think I will try to buy or rent a house in the country somewhere, and then you can come to see me. . . . I won't necessarily be with Jill, nice as she is. That remains to be decided. It will take me a long time to make up my mind. It may be that I would get to fighting with her all the time, too. So it might be wise of me just to hire a housekeeper and live pretty much alone except for visits from you and the rest of the gang.

Love—

K

After several setbacks at the mental hospital in Vancouver, Mark comes back to the Cape and begins his recovery by mowing lawns in the neighborhood, then starts taking courses in science and math at the University of Massachusetts Boston. Pleased to do well academically, he applies to medical schools. Out of the many he applies to, he is accepted by only one: Harvard Medical School.

When Sam Lawrence agrees to publish my first novel, *Going All the Way*, I ask him who my editor will be. Sam had made clear that he was "a publisher, not an editor." He said he always used his writers as the editors of his books.

"Who would you like it to be?" he asks me. "How about Kurt?"

I say that would be excellent.

You tell me later that you said to Sam that being an editor was a professional job, and you should be paid to do the job. When Sam asked you how much you wanted, you told him "an Eames chair."

I learn that an Eames chair is an expensive luxury chair with a hassock. Sam gets you one. As my editor, you write me a letter with ten suggestions you think could improve my novel. You add "Don't do any of these just because I suggested them. Only do the ones that ring a bell with you."

I do seven out of the ten and always remember the important advice: "Only do the ones that ring a bell with you."

***

You write to José Donoso on October 9, 1973:

> I hope that Jane will fall in love and marry again. She's still beautiful.
>
> I have become something of a public man. People recognize me sometimes, and I get a lot of invitations to speak. I turn most of them down. One I didn't turn down came from the American National Academy of the Arts, of which I am not a member. I got to deliver the main address at their annual meeting a couple of months ago. I was petrified.

Not only are you sometimes recognized by the man in the street, but you are finally awarded a master's degree in anthropology from the University of Chicago in 1971. They say they are giving it to you because they have decided that *Cat's Cradle* is a work of anthropological merit. Of course, *Cat's Cradle* came out eight years earlier, but back then you weren't yet recognized by people in the street.

***

March 20, 1972
To Mark Vonnegut

Dear Mark—
     . . . There is a screening of *Slaughterhouse* late this afternoon—for college people. I will be there to run a discussion afterwards. There will be no big premiere. The thing simply starts running at a theater three blocks from here on Wednesday, at noon. . . . My old war buddy, BV O'Hare, will be coming to New York to see the movie on Thursday. That will be a great adventure for me—watching him get his mind blown by a nearly perfect recreation of the past.

***

I am in New York that March and have lunch with you, and as we walk to the restaurant, you tell me how pleased you are with the movie that George Roy Hill has made of your novel. I am amazed that a good movie could be made of that novel, with all its movements through time and space. You stop and say with a smile, "They did it just like the movie of *Gone with the Wind*." You raise your arms in the air and make a gesture as if you are pasting something to a wall. You say, "They just took the book and put it on the screen."

Instead of trying to create a new plot, you explain, they just followed the scenes in the book. Not all the critics are crazy about it, but you are the rare writer who is happy with a movie that was made of your book.

***

Harper's Magazine commissions you to cover the 1972 Republican convention, which nominates Richard Nixon for a second term.

You soon tire of hobnobbing with the hotshots from the press and television and politicians from both parties who are yakking it up among themselves at lunches and dinners and drinks. You notice a group of people to whom no one is paying any attention; they are ten American Indians sitting by themselves on overstuffed furniture in the lobby of the convention hotel. On the coffee table in front of them are copies of a message that many Native Americans from many tribes have come to deliver to President Richard

Nixon. You seem to be the only person who has taken a copy of the message and read it. It says in part: "We come today in such a manner that must shame God himself. For a country which allows a complete body of people to exist in conditions which are at variance with the ideals of this country, conditions which daily commit injustices and inhumanity, must surely be filled with hate, greed, and unconcern."

You talk to the Native Americans. Mostly, you talk to Ron Petite, a Chippewa. He says nobody of importance will take the message from them. They are ignored. They see the president's daughters in line giving autographs, so they get in line and give their message to one of the daughters and ask her to give it to her dad.

It is extremely doubtful that Richard Nixon ever sees this message. It makes such an impression on *you*, at any rate, that you use a phrase from it as the title of your report on the Republican convention of 1972: "In a Manner that Must Shame God Himself."

* * *

The science fiction writer Harlan Ellison commissions you to write a short story for an anthology of original science fiction tales, *Again, Dangerous Visions*. The story you contribute to it is "The Big Space Fuck." You say it is your "farewell to the short story form."

You are named vice-president of PEN American Center, the United States branch of the international literary and human rights organization. This is not "an honorary position" for you. In this position, you carry on your lifelong battle against censorship in all countries. Your first experience with censorship was within your own family. Your cousin who owned a bookstore in Louisville always refused to carry your books. She, like many others, pointed to your use of the language of workingmen and soldiers and also your addressing controversial subjects.

∗∗∗

On August 29, 1972, you write to Mark with advice:

> I have mixed feelings about advances on first books. They are hard to get, for one thing, and they are usually so small that they tie you up without appreciably improving your financial situation.
>
> Also: I have seen a lot of writers stop writing or at least slow down after getting an advance. They have a feeling of *completion* after making a deal. That's bad news creatively. If you are within a few months of having a finished, edited manuscript, I advise you to carry on without an advance, without that false feeling of completion, without that bit of good news to announce to a lot of people before the job is really done. . . .

Thinking about money games now will simply fuck you up. Concentrate on creative games. That's your job. If your book makes a lot of money, which really good books usually don't, you will get that money as it is earned—in straight royalties. . . .

If you got a spectacular advance, then your royalties would be used to pay it off. You see? Same thing all over again.

And the hell with it. Write a book. . . .

Love and admiration—

K

***

On October 11, 1972, you write to Jerome Klinkowitz:

Dear Mr. Klinkowitz—

You have been most useful to me in caring about what I do. I mean that seriously. You have cheered me up. You have also exhumed work of mine that I had forgotten all about. In gratitude, I will send you various versions of my new book, *Breakfast of Champions*, which will be published next April or so. They will be your property. You can do as you please with them, such as they are.

Cheers,

Kurt Vonnegut, Jr.

Klinkowitz copies everything he can find that you have published—short stories, essays, book reviews, articles, anything by you. He is a professor of English at the University of Northern Iowa. He and another professor, John Somer of Emporia State University in Kansas, visit you and give you the copies of your work that they have collected. You have not kept copies of all of your own work. This collection that the young professors give you enables Sam Lawrence to publish a book of your nonfiction in 1974. The title of the book is *Wampeters, Foma and Granfalloons.* These words are ones you made up to use in your novel *Cat's Cradle.* A wampeter is "an object around which the lives of many otherwise unrelated people may revolve, such as the Holy Grail." Foma are "harmless untruths intended to comfort people." A granfalloon is a "proud and meaningless association of human beings." One example of a granfalloon is "Hoosiers."

***

You write to Jane on October 19, 1972:

Dear Jane—

I wish you a happy birthday in confidence that, American politics aside, it really will be a happy birthday for you. At the cost of unbelievable amounts of pain, you have bought a new life and a new Jane for yourself. You have always paid your dues, and you have paid them again. We've both always paid our dues. That's honorable. I still believe in honor, although I would play hell defining it.

Now that we are through the worst of our present adventure in a world we never made, in bodies we never asked for, with heads we only dimly understand, it seems safe to say that we hung on to more than most broken couples do. In a crazy way, it seems to me that we hung onto practically *everything*. We are not diminished.

I look forward to seeing you in November.

Much love—

K

***

On November 2, 1972, you write to Nanny:

Dear Nanny—

Good letter from you waiting for me when I got back last night from England. You have caught onto something I only learned in the past month or so—that terrific depressions are going to crunch me down at regular intervals, and that they have nothing to do with what is going on around me. . . .

Another thing which is inherited in our family: an ability to draw, and it is inherited only by females. Amazing. There is a line of women who were practically born drawing—going back and back and back.

Please send me a drawing.

Love—

K

November 2, 1972
To José and Maria Donoso

Dear Pepe & Maria Pilar—
    As for my happiness: I live from day to day and hour to hour. I know elation. I know despair. A doctor has prescribed pills for depression, which I take from time to time, as instructed. I still have life in me as an artist. I have finished another book [*Breakfast of Champions*]. It contains one-hundred and twenty drawings by me, as well as prose. My understanding is that I am so odd emotionally and socially that I had better live alone for the rest of my days. During my last years with Jane, there was a formless anger in me which I could deal with only in solitude. Jane did not like it. There is no reason why she should. Nobody likes it. What is it? Well—if I had to guess, I would say that it was caused by a combination of bad chemicals in my bloodstream and the fact that my mother committed suicide. I have finally dealt with that suicide, by the way, in the book I just finished. My mother appears in it briefly at the end, but keeps her distance—because she is embarrassed by the suicide. And so she should be.
    Love—
    Kurt

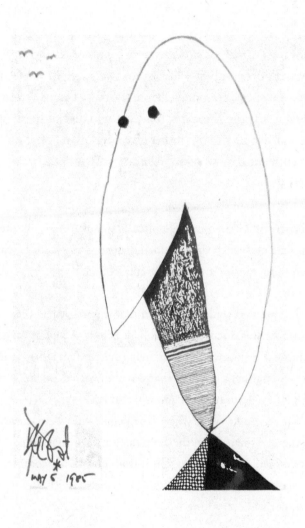

MAY 5 1985

* * *

In April of 1973, *Breakfast of Champions* is published and stays on the *New York Times* best-seller list for twenty-eight weeks. In this novel, you speak personally before the story begins as you did in *Slaughterhouse*. This time, however, you do not speak of your personal experience but rather give a lesson in American history, a correction to what we were taught in school.

You tell us:

> Teachers of children in the United States of America wrote this date on blackboards again and again, and asked the children to memorize it with pride and joy:
>
> 1492
>
> The teachers told the children that this was when their continent was discovered by human beings. Actually, millions of human beings were already living full and imaginative lives on this continent in 1492. That was simply the year in which sea pirates began to cheat and rob and kill them. . . .
>
> The sea pirates were white. The people who were already on the continent when the sea pirates arrived were copper-colored. When slavery was introduced on the continent, the slaves were black.
>
> Color was everything.

You originally set the story of *Breakfast of Champions* in Indianapolis, but you changed the setting to the fictional Midland City. You recognized the fate of authors who write about their hometowns when you said in your review of my novel *Going All the Way*, "Having written this book, Dan Wakefield will never be able to go back to Indianapolis; he will have to watch the 500-mile race on television." (Except for visits to parents and friends, I stayed away for more than fifty years.)

I am sure that your fictional setting of Midland City saves you from a lot of hostility from your hometown.

You introduce a new element in *Breakfast*—102 drawings you made for the book. They include a blimp that says "Goodbye Blue Monday," a flamingo, an apple, a tombstone, and other figures. It looks as if you had fun making these drawings. I can't think of any other novelist who would dare to do that and be supported in such an innovation by a publisher. Just as the drawings must have been fun for you, they are also fun for the reader!

And yet you deal with the most serious of subjects. "Suicide is at the heart of the book," you tell an interviewer.

It is also, you point out, "the punctuation mark to the end of many artistic careers."

You break all the standard rules of novel writing, so it is not surprising that many reviewers are put off by the book or surprising that so many readers make it a best seller. Who else dares to speak personally to begin a novel or to include their own drawings? It is important that you dedicate the book to Phoebe Hurty, who taught you to be impolite.

***

In May, you speak against censorship at the conference of International PEN in Stockholm. Honors are raining down on you. You are inducted into the National Institute of Arts and Letters; Indiana University awards you an honorary doctorate in the humanities. You begin a one-year teaching job as distinguished professor of English prose at the City University of New York. The writer Joseph Heller is teaching there also.

You buy a four-story town house on East Forty-Eighth Street between Second and Third Avenues in Manhattan. You work on the top floor; Jill has her office on the street level with a separate entrance. You share living space on the two floors in between.

In a letter to José Donoso on October 9, 1973, you write:

Vance . . . found you and Maria Pilar and Jane and Adam and everybody in a generally merry state. Hooray. I am naturally embarrassed by my separation from Jane, which has been interpreted as a faithless act. I think the passing years will make it apparent that she has been reborn into happiness and freedom which were inaccessible while I was with her. As for myself: after many black years, I, too, am becoming more resourceful and successful in the pursuit of happiness.

Cheers—

Kurt

Since you left Cape Cod, Jane has started going out with Adam Yarmolinsky, a Harvard professor who served in different capacities for the administrations of Kennedy and Johnson and will later serve in the Carter administration. He is in love with Jane and gets to know her children, doing his best to act as a father to them.

***

Knox sells an article Mark wrote to the *Village Voice*. Mark calls to tell me he is writing a book, and he says you told him that fathers are not the best people to be their sons' editors. You suggest to Mark that he show me the book. This seems right. I'll always remember seeing him bounding up the street to my house. I don't know how much editing we did, but we had a good time.

* * *

On November 16, 1973, you write to Charles McCarthy, the chairman of the Drake School Board of Drake, North Dakota. The school board burned copies of *Slaughterhouse-Five* in the school furnace.

> If you were to bother to read my books, to behave as educated persons would, you would learn that they are not sexy, and do not argue in favor of wildness of any kind. They beg that people be kinder and more responsible than they often are. It is true that some of the characters speak coarsely. That is because people speak coarsely in real life. Especially soldiers and hard-working men speak coarsely, and even our most sheltered children know that. And we all know, too, that those words really don't damage children much. They didn't damage us when we were young. It was evil deeds and lying that hurt us.
>
> After I have said all this, I am sure you are still ready to respond, in effect, "Yes, yes—but it still remains our right and our responsibility to decide what books our children are going to be made to read in our community." This is surely so. But it is also true that if you exercise that right and fulfill that responsibility in an ignorant, harsh, un-American manner, then people are entitled to call you bad citizens and fools. Even your own children are entitled to call you that.
>
> I read in the newspaper that your community is mystified by the outcry from all over the country about what you have done.

Well, you have discovered that Drake is a part of American civilization, and your fellow Americans can't stand it that you have behaved in such an uncivilized way. Perhaps you will learn from this that books are sacred to free men for very good reasons, and that wars have been fought against nations which hate books and burn them. If you are an American, you must allow all ideas to circulate freely in your community, not merely your own. . . .

Again: you have insulted me, and I am a good citizen, and I am very real.

Yours truly,

Kurt Vonnegut Jr.

The attempts to ban *Slaughterhouse-Five* and other books of yours are always defeated, as the American Civil Liberties Union successfully defends the book, citing the First Amendment to the Constitution.

* * *

Wampeters, Foma and Granfalloons, which collects your essays, articles, and book reviews, is published in May of 1974. This is the last of your works to be published under the name "Kurt Vonnegut, Jr." For subsequent works, you will use "Kurt Vonnegut."

In the summer of 1975, you rent a beachfront house in East Hampton, Long Island, and start to look for a second home around there.

Your uncle Alex dies on July 28 at age eighty-six. You write in a tribute: "I am eternally grateful to him for my knack of finding in great books reason enough to feel honored to be alive, no matter what else might be going on." Uncle Alex founded the Indianapolis chapter of Alcoholics Anonymous. You have said that you believe that America's greatest contribution to the world will be Alcoholics Anonymous. It was Uncle Alex who gave you a lesson that you never forgot and that you have passed on in many of your talks. Whenever you are aware of a nice moment, even a small one like having a glass of lemonade under a tree, you say to yourself, "If this isn't nice, what is?"

***

Mark publishes his memoir *The Eden Express*, which tells of his psychotic break and his recovery. The royalties from his book will pay his way through Harvard Medical School.

***

In 1976, Delacorte Press/Seymour Lawrence publishes your novel *Slapstick, or Lonesome No More!* The novel begins by speaking of the untimely death by cancer of your beloved sister, Allie, and goes on into a fictional autobiography of a man who has an adored sister. It fails to deliver what you and the reader hoped for. You report after its publication that the reviews are bad in the *New York Times*, the *New Yorker*, *Harper's*, the *Atlantic*, and "most other leading publications," and that some reviewers "actually asked critics who had praised me in the past to now admit in public how wrong they had been. I felt as though I were sleeping standing up in a Boxcar in Germany again." Despite all this, the book makes the *New York Times* best-seller list and remains on it for twenty-four weeks.

* * *

On April 6, 1976, you write to Jerome Klinkowitz, who has written you asking your advice about whether to accept a professorship at the State University of New York at Albany or to stay at the University of Northern Iowa.

Dear Jerry—

 I called my brother for his opinions on SUNY Albany, and learned that you had interviewed him only half an hour before. So now you have more substantial information than I do. . . .

 I am certain that you are highly valued and badly needed right where you are. That must be a nourishing situation. I envy it. If you move East, you may find that life becomes a lot less personal. You will become more of a floater. I myself am almost pure helium at the age of fifty-three.

 You have a strong sense of style, since you own an old Mercedes and play jazz on weekends. Since you have asked

my opinion, a foolish thing to do, I will tell you what I think
is the most stylish and useful thing for you to do. This is it:
Iowa is a better place than Albany. Stay where you are. . . .
Cheers—
Kurt Vonnegut, Jr.

Klinkowitz writes to his friend Donald Fiene at the University of Tennessee that this letter from you is "the most important thing he ever sent me, as it was life-changing. I stayed here and have been supremely happy, just as he suspected I'd be."

***

You write to Nanny on April 29, 1977:

Dearest Nanny—
Jane, who is fond of marriage, should have the chance to marry again. I am not pursuing happiness through divorce. I am permanently damaged by the break-up of marriage. Those wounds will never heal. I am simply trying to make the best of an unpleasant situation. Let me say again, too, that Jill did not break the marriage. It was broken long before that—about the time I went to Iowa. There was no other woman beckoning me to Iowa. Later on, there was no woman beckoning me to New York City. I arrived in both places in total solitude and feeling simply awful.

There will be no acrimonious argle-bargle about divorce this time. We will not make the mistake of hiring two strangers to fight each other on our behalf. Jane and I will arrive at some sort of division of property, and some scheme for my sending her money regularly. She already owns the Cape house and some stocks and a large savings account in cash. I will add to that treasure so she won't have much to worry about as long as I'm popular and productive. Then Don Farber will draw up a simple agreement, and that will be that. . . .

Love—

DAD

In the summer of 1977, you buy a second home in Sagaponack on Long Island. Your summertime neighbors include the writers Nelson Algren, Truman Capote, and Irwin Shaw.

***

On September 21, 1977, you write to José Donoso. You want to console your friend for getting a bad review in the *New York Times* from Anatole Broyard.

Dear Pepé—

Anatole Broyard has no constituency, is famous for reviewing only short books, and was kicked out as a daily

Goodbye and Goodbye and Goodbye

reviewer shortly before he did in your book in the Sunday *Times*. Things go badly for him. In effect, he has been busted from colonel to corporal. His response to the demotion has been an increase in bitterness in his reviews, and he will surely be busted again by and by. The publishers detest him. . . .

Cheers—

Kurt Vonnegut

***

You know that Sam Lawrence, like you, keeps the faith with Richard Yates, supporting him through disappointing sales, and you want Sam to know you are genuinely impressed with Yates's new novel, *A Good School*.

June 8, 1978
To Sam Lawrence:

Dear Sam—

Dick continues to be an immaculate artist with words and emotions. There is never a mistake anywhere. And what a nourishing conclusion he reaches in this book: That, by God, it really was a good school. I am so tired of people who examine their pasts and find nothing but mortal woundings. . . .

Cheers—

Kurt

* * *

On November 16, 1978, you write to Annie and Don
Farber:

Dear Annie and Don—

You two have given me many extraordinary gifts over
the years, but you have topped them all with Boris, the
chess robot. Perhaps you knew that Boris would be a highly
personal gift, since I once fancied myself quite a player. Mark
was the only person on Cape Cod who could beat me with
any consistency. You have refilled a great hole in my life. I
play several games a day again—at my own convenience, and
I love doing that.

I can beat Boris if I really concentrate—even when I give
him a full minute to make each move. But if I make the
slightest mistake, he is heartless, and I still can't believe the
brilliance of his end games. Really—he is one smart, mean
son of a bitch. The people who invented him must be ten
times as smart as Einstein. Five years ago, people were saying
that such a robot could never be built, since the variables in
each game ran into the billions. . . .

I have one small legal question. If Boris and I have a
falling out for some reason, can he sue for alimony?

Much love—

Kurt

* * *

In spring of 1979, you speak at the centenary of the Mark Twain House in Hartford, Connecticut. You say that America "would not be known as a nation with a simple, amusing and often beautiful language of its own, if it were not for the genius of Mark Twain."

On September 8, 1979, you write to Nanny:

> Dearest Nanny—
>
> I want you to be the first person in our family to find this out: That Jill and I have decided to marry each other in November, probably a couple of days after Thanksgiving. Jill will then be three months shy of being forty, and we will have lived together about nine years. . . .
>
> Some people, in telling of my adventures and mis-adventures of the past ten years, have made them conform to the conventions of a Gothic romance, with plenty of wickedness and goodness and innocence and cunning and high living and simple living and money and craziness. It hasn't been quite that lurid. . . .
>
> The attendants will be little kids—Jill's nieces and nephews, with her father giving her away, of course. It will be very private. We don't want our pictures in the paper. We will probably give a small party in a private room at some restaurant afterwards.
>
> As for the groom's side: I hope my brother will come. I

will do without a Best Man. I will be solo up there, without accomplices. I sympathize fully with the mixed loyalties you and all the rest of my children would feel on such an occasion. So I of course invite you all, and hope you all will come. If the ceremony and party are going to cause you pain, you should not subject yourself to that pain. Your coming or staying away will not be a vote for or against anything.

Mostly, dear Nanny, I want you to know how happy I am just now, and that I have every reason to look forward to some very good years ahead. We have all calmed down.

And remain assured that I love you as much as anybody on this planet.

YOUR FATHER

* * *

Your new novel, *Jailbird*, is published to good reviews. It deals with a good man who is caught up in the political scandals of his era—Watergate, the Vietnam War, and so forth. You manage to work in the story of one of your heroes, the radical labor leader Powers Hapgood.

On September 14, 1979, you write to Gail Godwin:

Dearest Gail—

I thank you for your kind remarks about *Jailbird*. We try to run a class operation here, but fail more often than not. The luckiest thing I ever did was to teach at Iowa for those two years. I picked up a very classy extended family that way. It made you and John and John and John and some others quality relatives of mine for life. I used to be in this trade all alone. Suddenly, I was a member of a really great gang. I never tire of asking you and the rest, "How goes it?" If you are ever in trouble, I will take you in. . . .

Love—

Kurt

***

Mark graduates from Harvard Medical School.

"Now that you're a doctor," you say to him, "tell me—what's the meaning of life?"

"To help each other get through this thing," Mark says, "whatever it is."

11.

NOVELS, ART SHOW, AND SERMONS

You have your first one-man art show of drawings and etchings at the Margo Feiden Galleries in Greenwich Village. You've always been proud of the drawing talents of your daughters, Edie and Nanny, and feel the art gene came down through your family, exhibited by your sister, Allie, in your generation. You have always drawn and doodled for fun, but you didn't use any drawings in your own work until the ones that were interspersed within the text of *Breakfast of Champions*. Making those drawings must have been fun for you—and they were fun for your readers, a treat that no novelist had dared before (or had the talent to bring off). The show at the Feiden gallery establishes your credentials as an artist.

You don't give up writing to devote all your time to art. You simply add your talent as an artist to your writing of books.

On December 20, 1980, you write to Donald Fiene:

> Dear Don—
> . . . As for the art show: I think people were surprised by
> how good it was. They were also wary about making fools
> of themselves by buying anything. I enclose a page from the
> October *Horizon.* Almost all of the 55 pictures for sale were
> on 14" by 17" [paper] . . . The price for that size was and
> remains $400.00. There were a couple of much bigger ones
> for $1000.00, and five littler ones for $200.00. We sold twen-
> ty-one in all. . . . I really tried to make wonderful pictures.
> This is no town for amateurs.

In January of 1980, you deliver your first sermon at the First
Parish Unitarian church in Cambridge, Massachusetts, on
the theme of human dignity. This does not mean you have
given up your identity as a "Christ-worshipping agnostic."
A few years later you will respond to a piece of mine in the
New York Times Magazine called "Returning to Church,"
which tells of my becoming a member of King's Chapel
in Boston, one of the few Christian churches in the Unitarian Universalist Association. The Sunday that the article
appears, I'll come home from church to find a message
from you on my answering machine.
"This is Kurt. I forgive you."

This will begin a long, good-humored, sometimes laughing and sometimes moving and thoughtful exchange on the subject of Christianity.

The Palm Sunday sermon you give at St. Clement's Episcopal Church in New York City reaffirms Ida Young's teaching: "I am enchanted by the Sermon on the Mount. Being merciful, it seems to me, is the only good idea we have received so far. Perhaps we will get another idea that good by and by—and then we will have two good ideas."

In 1981, you publish the collection *Palm Sunday*, which includes your Palm Sunday sermon (titled in the book "In the Capital of the World") as well as essays, articles, speeches, and reviews. You will follow that book with three new novels: *Deadeye Dick*, *Bluebeard*, and *Galápagos*.

***

Your work continues to be attacked by censors and book burners because you insist on using everyday language as it is spoken, and also in *Welcome to the Monkey House*, you address issues of sexual politics that are considered taboo.

In 1981, you write a letter to members of the American Civil Liberties Union:

Dear ACLU Member,

On April 21, 1970, a teacher at Jefferson Davis High School in Montgomery distributed copies of "Welcome to the Monkey House," one of my short stories, to her junior English class.

She was fired the next day for distributing "literary garbage."

The ACLU filed suit on behalf of the teacher, and on June 9, 1970, she was reinstated. Quoting from an earlier Supreme Court decision, the judge ruled:

"Our nation is deeply committed to safeguarding academic freedom, which is of transcendent value to all of us and not merely to the teachers concerned. That freedom is therefore a special concern of the First Amendment, which does not tolerate laws that cause a pall of orthodoxy over the classroom. . . . The classroom is peculiarly the 'marketplace of ideas.' "

Until very recently, there have been few attempts by school officials and others to censor library and textbooks.

Now, the book-burners are back.

Last June a group in Warsaw, Indiana, publicly burned 40 textbooks the school board had found to be "objectionable." Buoyed by public support, the school board then fired three teachers and dropped nine literature courses. A federal judge upheld the school board. The ACLU is appealing the case.

The American Library Association reports that complaints to public libraries have increased fivefold since the election.

Self-styled censors have undertaken a new national effort to rid classrooms and libraries of books of which they disapprove. . . .

I am offended as a citizen, as a writer, and as an ACLU member that certain elements are trying to drag us backward to the darker days of censorship.

The freedom to choose or reject ideas, to read books of our choice, and to publish freely is the very bedrock of our free society. The First Amendment is a prohibition of governmental interference with free speech.

I support the ACLU for many reasons but none as critical and important as its never-ending vigilance for free speech.

. . .

This is personally distressing to me because the ACLU is the only organization effectively fighting the censors.

I have never written a letter asking anyone to help a cause. Because I feel so strongly about what is happening in our country today and because I know the tremendous financial burden being placed on the ACLU, I have decided to do what I can to fight this ugly and dangerous trend. . . .

Sincerely,

Kurt Vonnegut

It is very unusual for writers to respond to book reviewers who have written bad reviews of their books. When I got my first bad review, I asked an early mentor, the Pulitzer Prize–winning journalist and columnist for the *New York Post* Murray Kempton, what I should do. Kempton said, "The only way to respond to a bad review is to point out any factual errors in a review—'this didn't happen on this date . . . that was not where it happened etc.' " If you are hurt by the reviewer's opinion, you swallow it and hold your peace. That is the code.

You break the code in the case of Anatole Broyard.

April 19, 1981
To Anatole Broyard

Dear Mr. Broyard—

I thank you for your comments on how slowly my literary reputation is dying. Part of the problem, surely, is that all my books remain in print, and people continue to give me credit for having written them. There is also the confusion caused by *Jailbird*, which was much too good to have been written by someone at my stage of decay, a red herring, you might say. I am presently working on yet another novel which may mislead readers into believing I should be counted among the living for yet a little while. How greedy of me. How tasteless. How pitiful.

As for *Palm Sunday*, it was quite openly loathed by your paper and some others, and was elsewhere praised with no embarrassment apparent to me. A stranger speaks well of me in *The Nation*, for example. Another did so in the *Los Angeles Times*.

Still, I am sure you are right that there are many critics who went to some trouble to say nice things about a book by me which they did not like at all. I can't name them, but I'm sure you can. I am sorry to have made them so uncomfortable, and that sentimentality or whatever required them to tell little white lies.

I am not a critic, but I can imagine what it must be like for a critic to remain seemingly respectful and friendly in the presence of a writer he knows to be all through, to be hollow, to be a man with a paper asshole, so to speak. Here is how I am able to imagine it, and here is how a lot of washed-up writers are able to imagine it—by analogy. A lot of us have found ourselves behaving respectfully and sympathetically and cordially and fraternally and so on when suddenly encountering, God forbid, Anatole Broyard.

Yours truly,

Kurt Vonnegut

You express the outrage felt by many fiction writers of the era who are upset about Broyard's habit of "overkill" criticism, especially toward male authors of his own generation. He got an advance for a novel from Sam Lawrence, who after many years of not seeing any novel from Broyard, asked him to pay it back. One of Broyard's main targets is the novelist Richard Yates, your friend and mine, on whom Broyard seems to take special vengeance; as well as attacking each of Yates's novels, Broyard goes to the trouble of writing a whole essay in the *New York Times Book Review* denigrating Yates's entire body of work.

Yates's theory of why Broyard has made such a mission of

dismissing his work is that in their early days in Greenwich Village, Yates and Broyard were rivals for the affection of a particular woman. Yates was the victor, and Broyard never forgave him.

The journalist Nat Hentoff writes an article in the *Village Voice* describing the unfairness of Broyard's reviews and asking the *New York Times* to no longer publish his criticism. Hentoff's view goes unheeded, though it is appreciated by many writers of the time.

All authors are concerned that many books are reviewed in an unbalanced manner both by friends and by enemies of the author. Reviewers are usually identified by books they have written or academic positions they hold. Yates says reviewers should be identified by their personal relation to the author; thus, he feels Broyard's reviews of his books should identify him as "a former rival for the love of the same woman."

Many authors' reputations are blessed by "the luck of the draw" of who reviews their book. You were lucky to have the *New York Times* assign the review of *Slaughterhouse-Five* to Robert Scholes, whom you knew at Iowa and who had praised your work in his book *The Fabulators*. Jack Kerouac was lucky that the regular *New York Times* reviewer who did not like the beat generation was on vacation when *On the Road* was published. By chance, it was reviewed by Gilbert Millstein, who lived in the Village and was very sympathetic to the beats. When the *New York Times* called me out of the blue and asked if I would review a new collection of articles and essays by a young writer named Joan Didion, I did not blurt out that she was a good friend of mine. I wrote a review with praise I sincerely believed.

You avoid being criticized for reviewing my book in *Life* magazine. Your first sentence of the review is "Dan Wakefield is a friend of mine." You continue, "I would praise his book even if it was putrid" (as far as I know, this is the only book review to use the word "putrid"). You go on to say that you would not give your word of honor that it was good unless you believed it was really good. You give your word of honor.

✳✳✳

Jane, who is living with Adam Yarmolinsky in Washington, DC, is diagnosed with cancer. Adam and Jane marry. You know that no matter what she faces, she will not fall prey to darkness. You write about her, "Jane could believe with all her heart anything that made being alive seem full of white magic. That was her strength."

✳✳✳

The writer Sidney Offit becomes your best friend in New York and your favorite companion for lunch. He is the editor of the Library of America volume *Vonnegut: Novels*

and Stories 1963–1973. He serves on the boards of the
Authors Guild and PEN American Center.

You write to him on December 18, 1981:

> Dear Sidney—
>
> I really miss you and all the other tennis pals. . . . You guys
> are the only friends I have. I am beginning to wonder if my
> arm will quit hurting and get strong again, the way the sports
> medicine doctor said it would. You went through the same
> thing, did you? . . .
>
> I was the person, incidentally, who asked Salinger to sign
> *Catcher in the Rye*, and who was refused most angrily. . . . I
> used Salinger's neighbor, the Centurian Frank Platt, to sign
> the book for its wonderful Russian translator, Rita Rait.
> Salinger not only refused. He stopped speaking to Platt. . . .
>
> Season's greetings—
>
> Kurt Vonnegut

* * *

In your 1982 novel, *Deadeye Dick*, a young gun enthusiast accidentally shoots a pregnant woman from miles away and tries
to find absolution. Writing a novel about the tragedies caused
by guns, even when people have no intention to harm, represents the long development of your attitude about firearms.
Your father had a gun collection, and you borrowed one to
take with you on your second western trek, the summer before

your senior year in high school. In your record of that "Rover Boys" adventure with your two buddies, you record one day that you went out looking for game, hoping to provide dinner for that night. No report was ever made that you or George or Bud shot anything worth cooking.

Whatever feelings of gun-toting romance you may have harbored, they were erased by the experience of World War II, and you became a passionate speaker against the bombings of Laos and Cambodia and the war in Vietnam, as you will be against the wars in Iraq. You told interviewer Israel Shenker in 1969, "I think people should be offended by so many things, beginning with the sight of a rabbit killed by a hunter."

You want to make clear that as a veteran of World War II and a POW, you never intend to speak against the veterans sent to fight these wars by our government.

On July 8, 1982, you write to Jack P. Wheeler:

> Dear Jack P. Wheeler—
> I respond to your letter of June 13 to Paul Moore [Episcopal bishop of New York], about my sermon at St. John the Divine. . . .
> I was praising the Vietnam veterans. I have always respected and praised them. This was perfectly clear to the congregation which heard my sermon. . . .
> Yours truly,
> Kurt Vonnegut

***

You are already the father to six children, but Jill has never had a child of her own, and after suffering a miscarriage, she is anxious to adopt a baby girl.

You write to Miller Harris about it on December 20, 1982:

> Dear Miller—
>
> . . . On Saturday we went to Philadelphia, where we picked up from an outfit called "The Golden Cradle" a three-day old girl which we are adopting. Her name is Lily. Jill wanted a baby so much, and I had no right to deny her one. I shall survive or whatever . . .
>
> Cheers—
>
> Kurt Vonnegut

***

On March 12, 1983, you write to Kathryn Hume, a professor of English at Penn State University and a literary critic.

> Dear Kathryn Hume—
>
> . . . I have been much encouraged by painters in believing that startling beauty could be achieved by broken rules. Really—modern painters have been my exemplars, and often

my friends. During my childhood in Indianapolis, local jazz musicians also excited me and made me happy. My relatives, meanwhile, were saying that jazz wasn't music at all. It sure sounded like music to me.

Cheers—

Kurt Vonnegut

* * *

You met Dr. Robert Maslansky in 1974, when he was director of medical education for Cook County Hospital in Chicago. He invited you to speak to his staff of young doctors, feeling they would benefit from hearing people with interesting ideas outside the field of medicine. He was pleasantly surprised when you said you'd be happy to do it, and when he asked you what your lecture fee would be, you told him "lunch." When Dr. Maslansky moved to New York to be medical director of addiction rehabilitation at Bellevue Hospital, he looked you up, and you became friends. You will write about him in your book *Fates Worse Than Death*, "Robert Maslansky, who treats every sort of addict at Bellevue, and in New York City jails too, is a saint."

You write to Maslansky on September 7, 1983:

Dear Bob—

. . . I have spent the summer trying to find out if I am smart enough to write about Darwinism as the dominant religion of our time. The results are inconclusive, and could hardly be anything else, since my I.Q. is (for New York City) a lousy 135.

I will be taking Mark and his eldest son Zack and my brother Bernard and one of his grown sons . . . blue-fishing off Block Island in a chartered boat this next weekend (September 10-11). After that, I will close up the country house and will be in town all winter. I intend to see a lot of you.

Cheers—

Kurt Vonnegut

* * *

The family bluefishing trips you host for almost a decade are usually all male (brother Bernie and his sons, Mark and his sons), but sometimes you like to invite Betty Friedan, author of *The Feminine Mystique*, the feminist book that was published in 1963 and rocked the complacent American patriarchy like a bombshell. You must have been the first male author to use her book as the catalyst for a fictional short story, in *Redbook* magazine in the same year. In "Lovers Anonymous," you spoof the book, using the title *Woman, The Wasted Sex or The Slavery of Housewifery*. You also spoof men's terrified reaction to the effect the book may have on their wives. When a man sees one of his buddies carrying the book, he warns him that if he lets his wife read it, "She'll walk out on you and the kids and become a rear admiral."

That seemed at the time an outlandish prospect—and a scary one to many American husbands. Nine years later the first woman admiral was sworn in by the US Navy. Friedan must have enjoyed the story.

More than twenty years after your story—and Friedan's book—appeared, you join her and actress Colleen Dewhurst at a press conference for the National Conference Against Censorship. After that, Friedan becomes a regular guest on your bluefishing trips.

* * *

February 13, 1984, is the thirty-ninth anniversary of the fire-bombing of Dresden. The nightmare of it strikes you again. You drink a lot and take too many sleeping pills and are hospitalized in what you call "the short-term nut ward at St. Vincent's Hospital." Your son, Dr. Mark, describes this as "a bizarre, surreal incident" but says, "It never felt like he was in any danger. Within a day he was bouncing around the dayroom playing Ping-Pong and making friends. It seemed like he was doing a not very convincing imitation of someone with mental illness."

On March 22, you write to your friend Walter Miller about the experience, reporting:

> Now I'm an outpatient, allowed to carry matches again. . . .
> As part of my therapy, I've rented a studio on MacDougal Alley

[in Greenwich Village], number 5, under the name of Asro. I go to work there every weekday now, just as though I had a job.

***

On April 18, 1984, you write to Ben Hitz, your friend since high school and the best man at your wedding to Jane:

Dear Ben—
. . . In two weeks, I depart for my first visit to Japan, for an international conference of P.E.N. in Tokyo. I have arranged to make a tour of potteries in the boondocks—in honor of my father, who would have rather been a potter than anything. He could have given up speaking almost entirely. That was a complaint that he often made: that people talked too much.
Cheers—
K

When your father retired from architecture, he moved to a cottage in Brown County, a picturesque part of Southern Indiana, where he took up the making of pottery.

***

On April 29, 1984, you write to Peter Reed, a professor in the English department at the University of Minnesota.

You credit him with collecting some of your early stories that you had not kept.

Dear Peter—

Always good to hear from you. You are a sort of flywheel on my reputation, mentioning me often even when I myself am as silent as a tomb. The Darwinian novel, *Galápagos*, has been a perfect son-of-a-bitch, since I have to be responsible as a biologist as well as a story-teller. I have taken the thing apart and reassembled it a thousand times. . . . I think maybe things are going a little bit better now. . . . I take a cab to work each morning, and then walk home every afternoon. The walk takes a lazy, window-shopping hour.

***

On February 12, 1985, you and Jill go to the world premiere of a new musical setting of the Requiem Mass of Pope Pius V promulgated in 1570 by decree of the Council of Trent. This is a big social event in New York, and hardly any of the people notice that the words to the Requiem Mass are printed at the back of the program in Latin and in their English translation. I would guess you are the only person to read the translation. You are appalled. You feel that the words are terrible and punishing, almost like the tortures of the Spanish Inquisition. The Mass begins with the words "Rest eternal grant them, O Lord, and let light perpetual shine upon them."

You think this is terrible. You think it would mean that your beloved sister, Alice, and all others who have died would get no sleep. You are so upset about the whole wording of the Mass that you go home and write your own version of the Requiem Mass. Instead of saying, "Let light perpetual shine upon them," your Mass begins with the words "Let no light disturb their peace." Eventually you publish your words to the Mass in your collection of nonfiction titled *Fates Worse Than Death*. In the next few years, you meet a composer who wants to set your words to music. You also meet an expert in Latin who makes sure that the words of the Mass you wrote are accurately translated from Latin into the English. Your words are set to music and performed by a Unitarian church choir in Upstate New York. Later your words will again be set to music when Susan Swaney, director of Voces Novae at Indiana University, commissions a number of composers to write music for your Requiem. It is performed at Indiana University.

In your new words to the Requiem, you refer to Jesus as "my wild and loving brother."

You always make it clear that you are not a Christian, but you demonstrate a deep appreciation of Jesus. You will tell the graduates of Agnes Scott College in a commencement speech:

> I say with all my American [Freethinker] ancestors, "If what Jesus said was so good, and so much of it was absolutely beautiful, what does it matter if he was God or not?

"If Christ hadn't delivered the Sermon on the Mount, with its message of mercy and pity, I wouldn't want to be a human being.

"I would just as soon be a rattlesnake."

***

In your 1985 novel *Galápagos*, you use a fictional trip to the Galápagos Islands to speculate about human evolution. You dedicate *Galápagos* to another important mentor of your teenage years, Hillis Howie, the Orchard teacher who took you on your first trek to the Southwest, which is still fresh in your memory all these years later:

In memory of Hillis L. Howie,
(1903–1982) amateur naturalist—
A good man who took me and my best friend Ben Hitz
and some other boys
out to the American Wild West
from Indianapolis, Indiana,
in the summer of 1938.

Mr. Howie introduced us to real Indians
and had us sleep out of doors every night
and bury our dung,
and he taught us how to ride horses,
and he told us the names of many plants and animals,

and what they needed to do
in order to stay alive
and reproduce themselves.

One night Mr. Howie scared us half to death
on purpose,
screaming like a wildcat near our camp.
A real wildcat screamed back.

* * *

In July of 1985, you come to a party to celebrate the publication of my novel *Selling Out*. The party is at a wonderful space in Central Park called the Dairy. Because this book is a fictionalized version of some of my Hollywood experiences in television, I am giving certain friends a toy statuette meant to resemble an Oscar, the award being given for "Friends Regardless of Ratings." I announce the names of the friends to come forward and receive my token award, and when I call your name, I see you at the back of the crowd. You shout, "Gangway!" and raise your hands to part the crowd. This is another word I have not heard for a long time (like "stuck-up.") It was often heard in the 1950s, when traveling outside America meant boarding a ship by walking up the gangplank, the ramp that led you on board.

* * *

On November 15, 1985, you write to Donald Fiene:

> Dear Don—
>
> . . . The best review [of *Galápagos*] so far was in *Punch*.
> Frivolous scientific speculation is an art form little appreci-
> ated over here. Critics who have come up through English
> departments don't like science mixed in with novels. They
> feel it should be kept in separate volumes, like *Lives of a Cell*
> and *The Double Helix* and so on. Victorians felt the same way
> about sex. It should be sequestered in manuals for specialists,
> they thought, it could so easily spoil a tale. . . .
>
> Cheers—
>
> Kurt Vonnegut

***

On December 16, 1986, Jane awakes from unconsciousness
and asks Edie to call her father. Edie later says, "I dialed
his number and put the phone on her ear. She was very,
very weak. It was a sweet conversation. Like old childhood
friends talking and she asked him how to leave the planet."

"I told her on the telephone," you later write, "that a sun-
burned, raffish, bored but not unhappy ten-year-old boy,
whom we did not know, would be standing on the gravel slope
of the boat-launching ramp at the foot of Scudder's Lane. He
would gaze out at nothing in particular, birds, boats, or whatever, in the harbor of Barnstable, Cape Cod. . . .

I told Jane that this boy, with nothing better to do, would pick up a stone, as boys will. He would arc it over the harbor. When the stone hit the water, she would die."

Three days later she left this life at eight o'clock that evening at her home with Adam in Washington, DC.

On December 28, 1986, you write to Helen and Walter A. Vonnegut, Jr.:

> Dear Colonel and Helen—
> Another story has ended: that of Jane Cox (Vonnegut) Yarmolinsky, who died after a five-year-bout with cancer of the abdomen on December 19th—at about eight o'clock in the evening. This was in her home in Washington, D.C. She was comatose, and simply stopped breathing, with close friends and relatives at hand. She was cremated the next day, and had a really swell funeral on Sunday, the 21st. My brother and I were there, and all six of her children with their mates, and three of her five grandchildren. She was a devout Episcopalian at the end, but the rules of that religion were broken for her funeral, in that there were eulogies—by her saintly husband Adam, and by three of her children, Mark, Nanny and Steve Adams.
> I thought you should know, since we were all so close in Chicago so many years ago.
> Much love—
> Kurt Vonnegut

You write to Peter Reed, a friend and literary critic, on January 20, 1987:

> Dear Peter—
>
> . . . I am about a month from finishing another novel—this one about an Abstract Expressionist painter in his seventies, looking back on the founding of that school of radical non-representation. It is called *Bluebeard* because he has a painting locked away which nobody is supposed to look at until he's dead. I wish to hell I knew what the book is *really* about. I should *know* by this time. My God—I'm on page 305! . . .
>
> Kurt Vonnegut

Your 1987 novel *Bluebeard* is a fictional autobiography of an abstract expressionist painter. Exiled to the house in Sagaponack, Long Island, at the time, you are surrounded by the former potato fields with old barns that painters of the 1950s like Jackson Pollock had converted into studios for their drizzling art. In the mood of that setting, you create your new character, painter Rabo Karabekian, and also an article on Pollock for *Esquire* magazine.

On March 5, 1987, you write to Donald Fiene about Stephen Jay Gould, a professor of zoology and geology at Harvard and one of the leading scientists of his time. Among his books is *Ever Since Darwin: Reflections on Natural History.*

Dear Don—

. . . I was glad to learn of Gould's mentioning *Cat's Cradle*.
We tend to like each other. We're both primitives, it seems
to me, Grandma Moses of the intellect. He came to hear me
lecture at M.I.T. a couple of years ago, and we had supper
afterwards. I was scared shitless of what he might say about
Galápagos, and didn't ask his opinion. But he dropped me a
note, saying it was pretty good science, and that the fur-cov-
ered human mutant is fairly common. . . .

Cheers—

Kurt Vonnegut

* * *

On January 16, 1989, you write to your friend Robert Weide
about some taped cassettes he sent you for Christmas of the
radio show of the comedy team known as "Bob and Ray."
Bob Elliott and Ray Goulding were on the air in different
formats for five decades. You are a great fan of their satirical
humor, which was full of spoofs and parodies.

Dear Roberto—

. . . The Bob and Ray stuff is one part of an adventure in
Jungian synchronicity which has enabled me at last to get going
on another book with some enthusiasm. For two years I wasn't
getting anywhere, and then those tapes gave me permission to be,
like them, intelligently ridiculous. Now I think I'm O.K. I sure

wouldn't have been O.K., though, if they and a couple of books, one on kinship and the other about the outbreak of World War One, hadn't arrived from nowhere in the nick of time.

Cheers—

Kurt Vonnegut

***

On April 23, 1989, you write to George Strong, one of the other American P.O.W.s who, like you, survived the fire-bombing of Dresden.

Dear George Strong—

I'm home again, to the extent that anybody's really got a home anymore. Maybe my fundamental home is in Dresden, since that is where my great adventure took place, and where one hundred of us selected at random were bonded by tremendous violence into a brotherhood—and then dispersed to hell and gone. Your seeking me out and greeting me like a brother was a profoundly important event for me. So I thank you for that.

. . . Joe Crone (Billy Pilgrim) died in Dresden, of course. And the nice Italian kid I mentioned, whose name I've forgotten, was accidentally shot by an Italian who had just found a loaded Luger in a ditch. So what are we up to: maybe fifteen per cent   now accounted for?

Fraternally yours,

Kurt Vonnegut

* * *

On April 25, 1989, you write to Don Farber about the death
of the wife of John D. MacDonald (referred to in the letter as
"John D."), a prolific writer of crime and suspense novels. He
was named the grand master of the Mystery Writers of America.

> Don—
>
> John D.'s wife died recently, as you probably know. The son is
> arranging a memorial service, and asking people like me to submit
> something to be read aloud there. This is my contribution.
>
> KURT

There are lots of good little families which go unnoticed
by even parochial little histories. One such had John D.
and myself and our dear wives as members, as children,
if you will, and with editors and agents in New York City
as parental figures. When we came home from the Second
World War, and having published nothing, we were determined to prosper by selling stories to the then exceedingly
rich and popular magazines. When I say "we," I include the
wives and eventually the children we had, since freelance
story-telling was and remains very much a family enterprise.
Without our mates, we would have sunk like stones. . . . So
we kept on and on. John D. achieved greatness, and so did
Dorothy. They were one flesh, and God love them.

   Kurt Vonnegut

You write to Robert Weide on November 13, 1989

Dearest Whyaduck—

. . . The important novelist Richard Yates and I used to deliver a highly unpopular joint lecture each semester at the Writers Workshop in Iowa City on the subject of how to survive in a Free Enterprise Economy by means of hackwork. We had both done a lot of that, without serious damage, seemingly, to our souls or intellects. Not that it felt good. . . .

The relief agency CARE sent me to Mozambique a few weeks ago, in an effort to get some publicity in this country about the hell Freedom Fighters have been making of that place since 1976. We flew from refugee center to refugee center in light planes, since the Freedom Fighters made Swiss cheese out of anything that dared venture out of town on a highway. There was a TV crew along, and they got a lot of footage of me looking at people who were slowly starving to death. . . .

Love as always,

Kurt Vonnegut

After going to Mozambique at the end of 1989, you wrote an article about your experience in *Parade*, a Sunday newspaper supplement magazine. You write about the experience in *Fates Worse than Death* that "if you color the people in old photographs of Auschwitz shades of brown and black, you would see what was commonly seen in Mozambique."

When you're writing your article about the trip, you get a room at the old Royalton Hotel in Manhattan and find yourself crying so hard you are barking like a dog. You didn't come close to doing that for World War II. The last time you cried and didn't bark like a dog was when Jane died.

12.

REUNION POSTPONED, ANTI-BOMBING SPEECH IGNORED

At last! You have evidently decided that your worldwide fame and success as a writer outweighs your negative assessment of your high school self as a "jerk" who was "unpopular" (in spite of being voted the second-most-popular boy in your senior class). You write to assure your old friend that you will attend and speak at the fiftieth reunion of your Shortridge High School class of 1940.

March 22, 1990
To Victor Jose

Dear Vic—

As far as I know I'll be there on June 16. My own views of the future are famously depressing. I would a lot rather talk about the past, or hear other people talk about it. But what the heck. Whatever you say. Again I am startled by how few of us have died. Whatever happened to the bell-shaped curve?

And I say again that my high school was better than any
college I attended, and I attended Cornell, Butler, Chicago,
and the University of Tennessee. . . .

Cheers,

Kurt Vonnegut

That spring, you also write to Ben Hitz:

I am now, because of my age and steadfast lack of faith, at
least a Bishop in my own religion, German Freethinking,
and am, in fact, treated as a peer by the likes of Paul Moore,
who has become one of my closest friends. I also get along
fine with Jesuits. It wasn't until I was sixty-four that I came
across a statement by Nietzsche that I could articulate why
committed Christians and Jews sometimes find me respect-
able: "Only a person of deep faith can afford the luxury of
skepticism."

Cheers and love to you, too. Our fiftieth reunion
approaches!

* * *

Oops! Saved by the bell! A case of Lyme disease keeps you
from attending your fiftieth annual high school reunion.
You may be the only person to regard Lyme disease as a
blessing!

You write again to Ben Hitz on July 25, 1990:

> Dear B.D. III—
>   . . . Lyme disease may have been a blessing. There would
> have been faces (once decoded from old age) at the reunion
> who would have reminded me of insulting and demoralizing
> times. . . .
>   Much love to you, old pal—
>   K

* * *

No matter how long you live, it seems you will never accept
the fact that your high school years were full of achievement and popularity—chairman of the Social Committee,
editor and writer for the Shortridge *Daily Echo*, winner
for the best act in the Junior Vaudeville, and second-place
candidate in the voting for "Uglyman," the most popular
boy in the senior class. And yet you insist on regarding your
high school self as if you were—to use Knox Burger's name
for a loser—Philboyd Studge.

* * *

Although you don't go to your high school reunion, you
go to Washington, DC, to speak about the firebombing
of Dresden at the National Air and Space Museum. It is

one of the series of lectures on "The Legacy of Strategic Bombing." You say:

> The firebombing of Dresden was an emotional event without
> a trace of military importance. The Germans purposely
> kept the city free of major war industries and arsenals and
> troop concentrations so that it might be a safe haven for the
> wounded and refugees. There were no air-raid shelters to
> speak of and few antiaircraft guns. It was a famous world art
> treasure, like Paris or Vienna or Prague, and about as sinister
> as a wedding cake.
>
> . . . Attacking a civilian population from the air, with or
> without warning, with or without a declaration of war, has
> become for most of us simply one more symbol, like the
> Liberty Bell, of national pride.
>
> Who could be so chicken-hearted as to say that the killing
> from the air of Muammar Qaddafi's adopted daughter, as
> well-intentioned as my own adopted daughter, was a serious
> matter, or even interesting? Not the *New York Times*. Not the
> *Washington Post*. Not MacNeil or Lehrer or Brokaw or Rather
> or Jennings [famous newscasters of the day].

You ask your seven-year-old adopted daughter, who is
sitting by an ex-POW, to stand on her seat as an approxi-
mation of what Qaddafi's adopted daughter was like before
we killed her with the very latest in air-to-ground weapons
technology. There is no press coverage of your remarks. You

are well known. The National Air and Space Museum is well known. The firebombing of Dresden is well known. With all this in combination, you would think some reporter might have found your remarks interesting.

"We got no press coverage," you later write, "in my opinion (although there was an overflow audience in the lobby watching on TV screens) because in Washington, D.C., citizens who say that air power has been or ever could be misused are regarded by those who decide what is news and what isn't as politically immature, like a lot of college kids and unlike Dr. Henry Kissinger, Nobel Laureate for peace. When all is said and done, we are simpleminded creatures, glad to believe on the basis of symbolism alone (up is better than down) that air superiority is moral superiority."

After your speech, a woman says to you, "Nobody should ever be bombed."

You say to her, "Nothing could be more obvious."

***

In June you go to the funeral of your war buddy and longtime friend Bernard O'Hare in Hellertown, Pennsylvania. You remember the first time you met him, at Camp Atterbury, in Indianapolis; he was reading a biography of Clarence Darrow, the great defense lawyer. You read laudatory obituaries of O'Hare calling him "one of the most admired and colorful attorneys in Northampton County."

***

On August 15, 1990, you write to Marc Leeds:

> Dear Marc—
>
> . . . In response to your question about the relationship of
> my style to jazz and comedians: I don't think about it much,
> but, now that you've asked, it seems right to say that my
> writing is of a piece with the nightclub exhibitionism you
> witnessed in Davenport, lower class, intuitive, moody, and
> anxious to hold the attention of a potentially hostile audi-
> ence, and quick (like a comic or a jazz musician) to change
> the subject or mood. . . .
>
> Cheers,
>
> Kurt Vonnegut

***

I happen to be in New York in January of 1991, and I go to
the Unitarian Church of All Souls on Lexington Avenue to
hear you speak against the First Iraq War (the US gives it the
kind of glamorous war-novel-y title that Mary O'Hare would
shake her head at: Operation Desert Storm). I later tell
someone who interviews me about you that "I never saw him
so angry as when he spoke against the First Iraq War." The
first half of that quote, "I never saw him so angry," is later
used alone to make it seem as if I'm saying that you were

angry in general during that period. When I saw you during that era when I was in New York, I never saw you angry at all. In assorted parts of your life, you had every reason to be angry, but you didn't inflict anger on friends.

I have lunch with you a few days after you speak against the First Iraq War, and over coffee we get to talking about World War II and the war that preceded it, the Spanish Civil War; that became a kind of testing ground for Hitler's air force, and a bombing of the city of Guernica shocked the world and inspired one of Picasso's most famous paintings, depicting the horrors of bombing undefined civilian populations (the painting *Guernica* hangs in the Museum of Modern Art in New York City in your time).

I say I knew a man who was in the Abraham Lincoln Brigade, the group of American volunteers who fought on the side of the republican government of Spain against the fascist forces of Franco. When I knew this man in New York in the fifties, he was teaching anthropology at Vassar.

"What was his name?" you ask.

"John Murra."

"He was in classes with me at the University of Chicago!" You suddenly get excited and call for the check.

"Let's go back to my house and call him!"

"Kurt, I haven't seen him in forty years or so."

You are undeterred. We hustle out of the restaurant and head for your house, hurrying to the phone. You ask me where he lives now.

"The last I heard, he was teaching at Cornell."

You call information in Ithaca and get a number for John Murra. It is the man we both knew, and now we are talking to him, exchanging greetings. That's all, but it delights you. It's as if we've accomplished a crucial mission.

Your delight in calling old friends out of the blue must date from the habit you describe in *Slaughterhouse-Five* of getting drunk "and then, speaking gravely and elegantly into the telephone, I ask the telephone operators to connect me with this friend or that one, from whom I have not heard in years."

But you can get just as big a kick out of it in the daytime, without even having a drink.

***

You learn at a party that Richard Yates is physically sick and broke, and you and some of his friends and admirers send money to his agent for a rescue fund. You hope that as well as receiving the money he needs, he is heartened by knowing he has a lot of admirers who care about him.

***

After a falling out with Jill over her infidelity, you write to your friend Robert Weide on June 12, 1991:

Dearest Whyaduck—

. . . I thank you for your richly supportive letters. . . .

I am ashamed of few things I have done in this life. But I can never forgive myself for giving darling, intelligent, good-hearted Lily such an awful mother. Lily is now eight.

As for marrying anyone else I will be 69 in November, and my father, who abused his heart and lungs with tobacco just as I have done, made it to 72, gasping and coughing for the last two years. So I would never ask any woman to commit herself to seeing me through that fast-approaching mode of departure. I feel fine, but it seems highly improbable that I really am fine.

This humiliating business with Jill has not only stopped my writing, which was going well. I can't even read a newspaper. Gutenberg might as well never have lived as far as I'm concerned.

Your continued friendship is most nourishing.

Kurt

***

Jill empties the house of your clothes and belongings and changes the locks on the doors so you can't get into your house. You take what you need to the house in Sagaponack, Long Island, and continue to write in the converted potato barn out there that once was the studio of a painter.

On July 7, 1991 you write to Billie Lyon, the wife of Ollie Lyon, your friend from the time you both worked as publicity writers for GE, with whom you remain lifelong friends.

Ollie says that his church life comes to mean more and more to him. Harvey Cox, the Harvard theologian, said that one of the most rewarding aspects of Christianity, when compared with other religions, was membership in a stable congregation. When I, an atheist (there's money in it), hear from a man about to get out of prison who has no family waiting for him, who wants to know what to do with his freedom, I tell him, "Join a church."   The risk in that, of course, is that he might join the wrong one, and wind up back in the cooler for blowing up an abortion clinic.

Cheers,

Kurt Vonnegut"

You write to Marc Leeds on January 16, 1992:

Dear Marc—

Rest assured that I think of you often, and that the bell you gave me is on my mantelpiece. I have been slow to answer your good letter of more than a month ago because my domestic life continues to be a shitstorm. My wife demanded a divorce, but then, as her love life failed to take the course she thought it would, she wants me back again. She thought she had another escort and meal ticket, but she was mistaken. Of all the words of mice and men, the saddest are, "It might have been." . . .

On occasion, Nature can be surprisingly merciful. It has always been the case with me that when my life is a mess I can find some relief by writing. So I am, after a year of hacking out trash on my IBM Selectric, at last in control of material which can be another novel. I feel good about it. It is called *Timequake*. Like this country, it should be completely finished in another year.

Cheers,

Kurt Vonnegut

Your use of the IBM Selectric, an electric typewriter, is as far as you give in to technology according to your friend Klinkowitz.

"He used to be opposed to electric typewriters," Klinkowitz tells me. "He said he liked the banging of the typewriter keys that you had to hit to get the words on paper. As far as I know, he never wrote on a computer. He loved sending his typed manuscript pages with his crossings out and written insertions of words to his typist on Long Island. He called her before sending more pages, and they discussed the birds she had seen."

Following your lead, Klinkowitz has written all his books on a typewriter. He did give into the IBM Selectric, but under your influence, he continues to be a devoted Luddite and never writes on a computer.

***

In May, the American Humanist Association names you "Humanist of the Year," and they also name you "honorary president of the American Humanist Association," a role in which you succeed the science fiction writer Isaac Asimov, who died in April that year. You give what I think is the best definition of "humanist" that I know: "We humanists try to behave as decently, as fairly, and as honorably as we can without any expectation of rewards or punishments in the afterlife. We serve as best we can the only abstraction with which we have any familiarity, which is our community."

You get one of your favorite jokes from the talk you give at the memorial service for Asimov. You tell me, "I forgot I was talking to an audience of humanists. I said, 'I know that Isaac is up in heaven now.'"

That elicits a wheezing laugh from you, and you say, "That rolled 'em in the aisles." Later you recount the story in your writing.

***

To use one of your terms, the "argle-bargle" with you and Jill continues. You remain in the Sagaponack house for the next two years but return to Manhattan to see Lily on school vacations.

***

The novelist Richard Yates, who you became friends with when you both taught at Iowa, dies on November 7, 1992, at age sixty-seven. I first met him in the Village in the 1950s but really came to know him when we both lived in Boston in the 1980s. I often had dinner with him at the Crossroads, a restaurant-bar in Back Bay that served as his headquarters. He spoke fondly of you and told me that when he was really down and out, he knew he could count on you for a loan of a couple thousand bucks.

I join you and many other admiring writer friends of Yates at a memorial service for him in New York City. People speak spontaneously about Yates, and you say, "He was just as good a writer as Nelson Algren, yet he never was as well known. Of course, Algren had an affair with Simone de Beauvoir [the French author of the worldwide feminist best seller *The Second Sex*]."

You pause for a moment and then add, as if in explanation, "These things count."

The roomful of writers bursts into laughter, recognizing the rarely spoken truism that literary reputations are enhanced by that kind of publicity. You can't help speaking the truth.

***

You write to Knox Burger on May 7, 1993:

Dear Knox,

That's something nice I'd given up hoping for, an easy and friendly letter from you. The brutality of the choice I was forced to make between you and Max is now as little remembered, thank goodness, as Shays' Rebellion or whatever. . . .

For the sake of our darling adopted daughter (half Jewish, half Ukrainian, kind of like you, now that I think about it), Lily, now ten, Jill and I are not divorced. I am too old, anyway, for all the paperwork. Divorce has become as obsolescent as marriage. . . .

I was awarded a Lifetime Achievement Award by an arts support outfit in East Hampton a couple of years ago, and I said in my acceptance speech, "Does that mean I can go home now?" I wish I knew where home was.

Cheers (as Max used to say),

Kurt Vonnegut

* * *

In another of the fortunate encounters that injects some much-needed "zowie" into your life, you accept an invitation from your old friend from GE days Ollie Lyon to give a benefit reading and talk at Midway University in Midway, Kentucky. You are asked to collaborate with a local printmaker, Joe Petro III, for a collectible poster with a limited edition for the event on November 1.

You send him a black felt-tip pen drawing of your profile, and Petro makes it into a colorful silk-screen print.

You go to see the thirty-seven-year-old Petro at his studio, and the two of you form a partnership, the Origami Express. You and Petro will produce numbered, limited-edition prints based on your drawings. This becomes a lasting partnership, and it gives the kind of zap to your artwork that Iowa gave to your writing.

As you proclaim more than a decade later (and more than two hundred discrete Origami editions of silk screens later), "One of the best things that ever happened to me, a one-in-a-billion opportunity to enjoy myself in perfect innocence, was my meeting with Joe."

* * *

At the start of 1994, Seymour Lawrence dies at age sixty-seven. You have often said that he saved you "from smithereens." You write of him now in tribute: "That anything I have written is in print today is due to the efforts of one publisher. When in 1961 I was broke and completely out of print, Sam Lawrence bought the rights to my books for peanuts, from publishers who had given up on me. Sam thrust my books into the myopic public eye and made my reputation."

∗ ∗ ∗

You write to Paul Cody, an associate editor of the Cornell alumni magazine, on January 25, 1994, in response to his asking a number of alumni and friends of the university, "At this stage of your life, knowing what you know now, what advice would you offer to your graduating from college self?"

Dear Paul Cody—

. . . Advice? Somebody should have told me not to join a fraternity, but to hang out with the independents, who were not then numerous. I would have grown up faster that way. Somebody should have told me that getting drunk, while fashionable, was dangerous and stupid. And somebody should have told me to forget about higher education, and to go to work for a newspaper instead. That is what a lot of the most promising and determined young writers used to do back then. Nowadays, of course, you can't get a job on a newspaper if you don't have a college education. Too bad.

My experiences at Cornell were freakish in the extreme, as have been most of those which followed, mostly accidents. So the advice I give myself at the age of 71 is the best advice I could have given myself in 1940, when detraining for the first time at Ithaca, having come all the way from Indianapolis: "Keep your hat on. We may end up miles from here."

Cheers,

Kurt Vonnegut

***

You are asked by Dan Simon, publisher-editor of the newly
founded Seven Stories Press, to write an introduction to
a new edition of Nelson Algren's 1942 novel, *Never Come
Morning*. You appreciate Simon's commitment to the work of
Algren, whom you've always admired. You like that this new
independent publisher is committed to issues that are dear
to your heart: social justice, human rights, and progressive
politics. You agree to serve as an advisory editor to the press.

***

At the end of 1995, you finish a draft of the novel
Timequake, based on the concept that there is a glitch in
the space-time continuum and everyone has to live the
decade of the nineties over again doing the same things
and making the same mistakes. That description is awfully
solemn, though, and does not really convey the lively
stories that come together in what you describe as "an auto-
biographical stew." When you send your rewrite to Putnam
a year later, your editor complains that "it's not a novel."
You send it to your old friend Klinkowitz, who thinks it's
some of your best work. You explain that your publisher
complains that it's not a novel.

"Tell them it's 'the autobiography of a novel,'" your
friend advises.

Reunion Postponed, Anti-Bombing Speech Ignored

The publisher like the idea. "The autobiography of a novel." That has class! They buy it.

***

You write to Peter Reed on January 6, 1996:

> Dear Peter—
>   When I teach creative writing, I make Vincent van Gogh the class hero, since he responded to life rather than to the marketplace, and the class motto is: "Whatever works works."   . . .
>   The filming of *Mother Night* in Montreal ended, with everybody pleased, on November 10th. . . . Unbelievably, it was made for five and a half million dollars! Nolte [the actor Nick Nolte] himself usually gets paid much more than that. When he saw Weide's script, he said it reminded him of why he became an actor.

***

Your brother, Bernard, dies on April 25, 1997, at the age of eighty-two. He was the recipient of twenty-eight patents, and the American Meteorological Society recognized him by giving him the award for Outstanding Contribution to the Advancement of Applied Meteorology for pioneering discoveries in weather modification.

On May 5, 1997, you write to Harry James Cargas:

> Dear old friend Harry—
> I thank you for your condolence note about my brother.
> He didn't call for a priest at the end, but he had the good
> sense to spend the last ten days in a Catholic hospice, St.
> Peter's in Albany. One person there described his manners
> while dying as "courtly" and "elegant." I myself said at the
> memorial service last Thursday, in the non-denominational
> chapel of SUNY Albany, "I don't have anybody to show off
> for anymore." . . .
> Cheers—
> Kurt Vonnegut

***

Your novel *Timequake* is published in September and is
received with good reviews. *Newsweek* says it's your "fun-
niest book since *Breakfast of Champions*," and the *New York
Times Book Review* calls it "a blessing."

***

It turns out that you, unlike Melville's whalers, still have a
few things to say! In 1998, radio station WNYC-FM commissions you to write a series of ninety-second radio skits
in the form of satiric reports on the afterlife. You imagine

yourself in a "controlled near-death state" induced by Dr. Jack Kevorkian. You imagine yourself interviewing such luminaries as Sir Isaac Newton, Eugene V. Debs, and Mary Shelley. You expand the best of the skits, and they are published as an eighty-page book called *God Bless You, Dr. Kevorkian*, published in 1999 by Seven Stories Press.

***

On November 7, 1999 you write to Ms. Noël Sturgeon, the fourth daughter of Theodore and Marion Sturgeon and the trustee of Theodore's literary estate. Many readers are curious about the relationship between your character Kilgore Trout, the science fiction writer, and Ms. Sturgeon's father, a well-known and highly regarded science fiction writer.

> Dear Ms. Sturgeon—
>
> I created a character Kilgore Trout, an impoverished, uncelebrated science-fiction writer, who made his debut in 1965, in my novel *God Bless You, Mr. Rosewater*. Trout would subsequently make cameo appearances in several more of my books, and in 1973 would star in *Breakfast of Champions*.
>
> Persons alert for word-play noticed that Trout and Theodore Sturgeon were both named for fish, and that their first names ended with "ore." They asked me if my friend Ted had been my model for Kilgore.

Answer: Very briefly, and in a way. Kilgore, like Ted when we first met in 1958, was a victim of a hate crime then practiced by the American literary establishment. It wasn't racism or sexism or ageism. It was "genreism." Definition: "The unexamined conviction that anyone who wrote science-fiction wasn't really a writer, but rather a geek of some sort." A genuine geek, of course, is a carnival employee who was displayed in a filthy cage and billed as "The Wild Man from Borneo."

Genreism was still rampant in late autumn, 1958, when I was living in Barnstable, on Cape Cod, and Ted and his wife Marion had just rented a house near the water in Truro—no place to be when winter came. We knew each other's work, but had never met. Bingo! There we were face-to-face at last, at suppertime in my living room.

Ted had been writing non-stop for days or maybe weeks. He was skinny and haggard, underpaid and unappreciated outside of the ghetto science-fiction was then. He announced that he was going to do a standing backflip, which he did. He landed on his knees with a crash which shook the whole house. When he got back on his feet, humiliated and laughing in agony, one of the best writers in America was indeed, but only for a moment, my model for Kilgore Trout.

Respectfully yours—

Kurt Vonnegut

* * *

You write to Nanny to bring her and the rest of the family up to date:

It really was a fancy spill I took up that way, most of all reminding me of how old I was. The black eye is vanishing. . . . now it's cold out, but I have a bed here, and a kitchen downstairs.

Most of all, I have done all I could to keep Lily out of a lockdown, punishing school, where she can be put away, pretty much out of sight, until she's eighteen. And I got lucky, since Jill, providing an alternative scheme to Northampton as quickly as possible, discovered a great little private school in a townhouse only two blocks north of here—The Beekman School. It is for good kids like Lily who have gotten into some sort of not-so-terrible teen-age trouble. There is heavy one-on-one tutoring. Ninety percent of the graduates go on to college. There is now only one other kid in Lily's English class! And it isn't all that expensive, much cheaper than Cushing Academy. I had no idea such a sweet institution existed so close to home. Lily likes it a lot, and it likes Lily.

I am living one day at a time, and I have to, Jill is so volatile. A Christmas and New Year's vacation in a beachfront cottage on St. Barts was planned and paid for (no refunds) almost a year ago. There are three airplane tickets, and it is now understood that I will not use one of them, but that Lily can bring a friend along in my place. I pray this really happens. Jill, as punishment for some very slight offense, could easily cancel so as to sicken me and make Lily cry. Departure date is December 22nd.

Love—

DAD

You write to Nanny again on December 14, 1999:

Dearest Nanny—

. . . When I got back to this city all bunged up, and realizing that I was 77, for God's sake, and having been told that Jill would do all within her power to prevent Lily's going to Northampton High, and that Jill had found what is really a good school for Lily, which we didn't know existed, only two blocks away, I went to bed in a bed which had been mine for years, in a room where all my things were. I was exhausted and actually injured, and so gave myself what was unavailable from anyone else, which was TLC.

Jill and I are not speaking, thank goodness, and I am on the mend and Lily has begun to recapture the lost half of her junior year, and has made a lot of new friends. . . .

And I am not about to turn off the ignition. I could never do that to the rest of you.

Love as always—

DAD

***

In the midst of all the argle-bargle with Jill, Peter Reed of the University of Minnesota puts together a book of the twenty-three stories of yours that weren't been collected in *Welcome to the Monkey House*. It turns out you have something to say about the stories and the era in which you wrote and how different it is for writers starting out today. In an introduction to the book, you have even more to add about other things on your mind, including your roots in the Midwest, so you add a coda, which, along with Peter Reed's preface and the twenty-three stories, makes for a very enjoyable book called *Bagombo Snuff Box*. It makes a sweet farewell to the twentieth century.

13.

A MAN WITHOUT A COUNTRY, SOMETIMES WITHOUT A HOME

The millennium does not get off to a promising start for you. Ensconced on the top floor of your house in Manhattan with a bed, books, TV, and laptop, you are watching the Super Bowl between the St. Louis Rams and the Tennessee Titans, smoking your usual Pall Mall, when you go down to scare up some food and forget about the burning cigarette. A neighbor sees smoke belching out of your fourth-floor window and bangs on the door of your house. The two of you run upstairs to find the room filled with smoke, and you try to save some of your papers. The fire department arrives, and you're carried out of the house on a stretcher and taken to the emergency room at NewYork-Presbyterian Hospital.

Two of your Adams sons come down to New York and take you to Northampton, Massachusetts, where you will be near your daughter Nanny. A rental apartment is found for you in the home of one of Nanny's friends.

From Northampton, you write to Knox on March 25,
2000:

Dear Knox—

How sweet it is to hear from you, old friend, and to know
that bygones are really bygones. I worry about your health.
Your warm letter finds me writing a tribute to Joe Heller, to
be read at the academy on April 4th. That will be my first
return to Manhattan since a fire in our brownstone ruined
only one room on Superbowl Sunday. But in that room,
lost to me now, were my papers, books, bed and clothing,
including my tuxedo. Jill's and Lily's quarters and the rest of
the house, save for minor water and smoke damage, are still
okay, but Jill doesn't want me back until repairs are made.
The property is generously insured, but Jill has yet to let
in workmen. And yes, good old Knox, I am a neighbor of
relatives, my daughter Nanny and the three Adams brothers,
who drive me on errands and otherwise take good care of me.

From Northampton, you write to Miller and his wife
Mary Louise Harris on April 28, 2000:

You have been so supportive as I muddle through this new
adventure. Battle of the Bulge indeed. But not really, except
that the weather has been terrible. I now have four of my
six middle-aged children within a radius of only 20 miles,
and the other two, one in Boston and the other on Cape

Cod, are coming to check up on me this weekend. I am getting divorced, and have a one-year lease on the above property, and expect to do some teaching at Smith, and maybe Amherst, too, when the leaves turn to gold. I read the obituaries in the *New York Times*, and all those making their departures are in their eighties and nineties now. Merde!. . . .

There will be a show of about forty of my silk-screen pictures in a gallery here next October or so. The foliage itself is worth a trip that time of year.

Love—

Kurt

On June 4, 2000, you write again from Northampton to Miller and Mary Louise Harris:

Dearest of Old Friends—

Your unexpected and typically unstinting gift to me of finest raiment put me in mind of Napoleon in exile on Elba. I am taller than he was, but I know as he did what it was like to be a Corporal and then to be ousted from scenes of triumphs in later years. My own Corporalcy was a brevet rank, awarded shortly before my discharge. I don't know about his. His quarters on Elba were reasonably comfortable, as are mine in Northampton—and he too must have received well made and tasteful gifts like yours from those who still thought well of him. Smoke and flames in my face from a fire possibly but not certainly caused by my own careless disposal of smoking materials were my own Waterloo. In any case, Napoleon was humbled, and so am I. Come see me! I have a guest room with its own sanitary facilities indoors. Do you suppose Napoleon had to use a privy out back?

Smith College is only two thousand yards from here, and I expect to teach "creative writing" there next fall. Can do!

* * *

On June 15, 2000, you return for your sixtieth reunion at Shortridge. The jocks didn't believe you would come, saying you were too much of a hotshot celebrity. You come, though, and stay with your old friend Majie Failey. You are there as your old O.W.L.S. club friend, Vic Jose, opens the ceremonies at the Woodstock country club on Friday, June 16. The next night is a great party at the Athenaeum, the landmark building designed by your grandfather. The class of 1940 commissioned Mary Weide, the sculptor wife of your long-time friend Bob Weide, to create a bronze bust of you. "The Kurt Vonnegut Room" in the Athenaeum is christened with the presentation of that sculpture and remains there to this day. At last, you have to accept that you were not a "jerk" in high school and are still beloved by your classmates, who are proud of your achievements. Your main jock tormentor has not come to see you honored by the class.

When you speak to the class on Saturday night, you do not come on like a hotshot from New York. You begin by

singing "That Old Gang of Mine" and end your talk by
telling them:

> There is a snide saying: "The big dreams go to New York;
> the little dreams stay home."   The biggest dreams, in fact,
> stay home. They build cities like this one with hospitals and
> universities and libraries and theaters and concert halls and
> supremely civilized gathering places like the Athenaeum. I
> say to all stay-at-homes, "Congratulations."
> Dream on, dream on!

* * *

You return to Sagaponack when you get back to New
York and start a new novel about a stand-up comedian
entertaining the country during the last days of human
existence.

You accept a position as writer in residence at Smith College in Northampton, working with a few fiction writing
students and giving some talks at Smith and other nearby
colleges in western Massachusetts.

You write to Knox Burger on March 6, 2001, from
Northampton:

> Dear Knox—
> I remember you. Didn't I dedicate a book to you one
> time? . . .

I myself am all alone and as celibate as any hetero-sexual Roman Catholic priest, in a spiffy apartment in Northampton . . . where the only African-American resident is my boss Ruth Simmons, the president of Smith. Maybe you heard she's going to be president of Brown next year. A twofer! Her PhD is in French literature. . . .

A guy is now writing a biography of Dick Yates, and he called me. I told him about the time Yates set his bed on fire, and I visited him in the burn ward at Bellevue, and he asked me for a cigarette. I asked the biographer if he had read *Winnie the Pooh*. He had, and I told him Dick Yates was Eeyore. . . .

I still smoke like a house afire, having at last actually set my house afire. That's why I came up here, to be near my daughter Nanny and my three adopted nephews, while recovering from smoke inhalation. I am suing Brown & Williamson. They promised to kill me on every pack of Pall Malls, but here I am, having accepted an enormous advance from Putnam for a book I can't write. My efforts reek of ennui. . . . It would be a tremendous relief to have supper with you and Kitty and the Harrises during Smith's spring break, which begins on the fifteenth of this month. I will be in New York and will give you a ring.

Cheers—

Kurt Vonnegut

***

You write to the editors of the *New York Times* on September 12, 2002, from New York City:

> Dear Editors:
> It may give us some comfort in these worrisome times to know that in all of history only one country has actually been crazy enough to detonate atomic weapons in the midst of a civilian population, turning unarmed men, women and children into radioactive soot and bonemeal. And that was a long, long time ago now.
> Yours truly,
> Kurt Vonnegut

* * *

In January of 2003, the editor of *In These Times*, a biweekly newsmagazine based in Chicago, interviews you about the coming US war in Iraq. You share the political views of the editor, Joel Bleifuss, which are in sync with the progressive tradition of your fellow Midwesterners Eugene V. Debs and Powers Hapgood. You become a columnist for *In These Times*, publishing essays, drawings, humor pieces, and fragments from the novel you started about the end-of-days stand-up comedian, now titled *If God Were Alive Today*.

* * *

You send me one of your silk-screen drawings dated
October 20, 2003. It is a black and red drawing called *Wasp
Waist*, and written at the top is a dedication: "Dear Dan
Wakefield, Unitarian-Universalist Fanatic."

You explain that since I am a Christian within the largely humanist Unitarian Universalist Association, which is primarily humanist, I must be a "fanatic."

In 2006, you and Jill come to hear me speak at St. Bartholomew's Church in New York City about a new book I have published called *The Hijacking of Jesus*. After the talk, Jill goes back home, and you take me to dinner across the street at the bar of the Waldorf-Astoria. You are having your usual predinner Manhattan and I my glass of red wine when one of the pair of young men who have been staring at you from across the room comes over and asks, "Are you the real Kurt Vonnegut?" You admit your identity, introduce him to me, and puff my new book (which the young man has no interest in whatsoever) and after politely answering a few questions, you give him a salute, and he thanks you and goes back to his table.

Later that year, I get a large package from you, this one containing a beautiful framed "poster" you have made for me with a golden flower at the center and these words:

BLESSED ARE THE HAPPY-GO-LUCKY GIRLS AND BOYS.
A NEW BEATITUDE FOR MY CHRISTIAN FRIEND DAN.

I call to thank you and say, "What do the words mean in the new beatitude you sent me?"

"Someone showed me a French translation of the Bible," you say, "and instead of 'Blessed are the meek,' it says,

'Blessed are the *debonair.*' I translated 'debonair' to mean 'the happy-go-lucky boys and girls.' "

You say, "I never liked the word 'meek' in 'Blessed are the meek'—it reminds me of a 'hangdog' kind of people."

I am very happy to have your new beatitude.

BLESSED ARE THE HAPPY-GO-LUCKY GIRLS AND BOYS.

A NEW BEATITUDE FOR MY CHRISTIAN FRIEND DAN KV 1/18/06

unused

y

***

In 2005, Seven Stories Press brings out a collection of the best of your recent essays, *A Man Without a Country*. Jon Stewart interviews you on *The Daily Show*, introducing you to a new audience (young audiences have always been your fans), and the book becomes a hit, making the *New York Times* best-seller list. I am not surprised. The book captures the essence of your work, making us want to laugh and cry at the same time.

***

On February 6, 2007, from New York City, you write to Professor Alice Fulton, an American poet and a member of the faculty at Cornell University:

> Dear Professor Fulton:
>
> I am of course honored by your invitation and praise of my work, and especially since your department at Cornell is said to be a strong one, as it was in my time there, Class of 1944. Unfortunately back then I was majoring in chemistry, at the insistence of my father: '"Learn a trade!"
>
> In any case, I cannot be of any use to you and your students nowadays, alas, since, at 84, I resemble nothing so much as an iguana, hate travel, and have nothing to say. I might as well send a spent Roman candle in my stead.

So no gig there, for want of a performer.

I scarcely write anything anymore, save for letters like this one. I'm making pictures, though, which my partner turns into silk-screens. . . . If you are curious about their nature, you can find some of them at www.vonnegut.com. I myself can't find them that way, since I don't have a computer, nor a cell phone, nor even an answering machine.

But God bless you for being a teacher.

Cheers, dear Alice, also my sister's name.

Kurt

* * *

The following month you fall on the steps of your town house and hit your head on the pavement, knocking yourself out. You are taken to the hospital but never regain consciousness. You leave your beloved green orb on April 11, 2007, at age eighty-four.

These were the last words of advice you wrote, meant to be delivered to an audience the following week in Indianapolis to begin "The Year of Vonnegut" in your old hometown: "And how should we behave during this Apocalypse? We should be unusually kind to one another, certainly. But we should also stop being so serious. Jokes help a lot. And get a dog, if you don't already have one. . . . I'm out of here."

THE END

ACKNOWLEDGMENTS

After I had begun the final work—the principal work—on this manuscript, I learned that my failing eyesight was due to macular degeneration. It is not a nice disease for a writer. It is sort of like polio for a distance runner.

Before I was aware of the dimensions of the disease, I realized I needed a new student assistant. My last excellent student helper had gone to get her MFA in Urbana, Illinois. I called my next-door neighbor and friend, Karen Kovacik, a professor of English at IUPUI (the awkwardly named Indiana University–Purdue University Indianapolis, which Vonnegut suggested might more happily be called "Stardust University," for the song written by our fellow Hoosier Hoagy Carmichael).

Karen said she would think about it and get back to me. The next day I was going out to pick up the newspaper on the sidewalk in front of my house when I heard Karen shout from her front porch, "Does gender matter?"

I said, "Well, it's always been female," and as soon as I said it, I knew that was the wrong answer.

The next day, Karen called and said there was one student who was much like my former helper, but she was very busy with courses and other work and might not have the time. The next three best students for the job, she said, were all trans.

In two seconds, my whole life flashed before me. My first thought was "Oh, God, does this mean I have to learn some new kind of vocabulary at age eighty-nine?" My next thought (in the following second) was "You jerk, are you forgetting that it took you a whole lifetime to get over your mother complex and all its attendant hang-ups? How could you not be sympathetic to anyone trying to forge for themselves their own true identity?"

"OK," I said to Karen. "Who's the best of the three?"

"Nate," she said.

"Then I'll take Nate."

That was the luckiest decision of my last several decades.

I could never have finished this book without Nate Marquam. I don't mean just because his eyesight is so much better than mine.

Once while I was going over the manuscript with him and listening to one of his comments, I suddenly asked, "Have you ever thought about living in New York City?"

"Why?"

"Because you could have a great career as an editor," I said.

At this point, Nate plans to be a teacher. I am sure he

would be just as good a teacher as an editor. Or many other choices. As Kurt liked to say, repeating the wise words of a salesclerk, our children are "hostages to fortune."

God bless them all. God bless Nate. And thank you, Karen.

* * *

My good fortune is to have such good and faithful friends, including scholars and writers whose aid was crucial. This book began in conversations with Dr. Mark Vonnegut, my friend since the days when he was writing his first memoir, *The Eden Express*. I have used material from that book and from his next powerful memoir, *Just like Someone without Mental Illness Only More So*, the best account of growing up with Kurt and Jane, which he likened to "being raised by wolves."

I met Jerome Klinkowitz in 1972 when he came to Boston to ask me to contribute to a collection he was editing called *The Vonnegut Statement*. A professor at the University of Northern Iowa, Jerry, along with another professor, John Somer of Emporia State University in Kansas, had collected all things Vonnegut had written—stories, essays, reviews—and delivered them to him, and they had formed the contents of Vonnegut's first book of essays, *Wampeters, Foma and Granfalloons*. Klinkowitz's books on Vonnegut, *Vonnegut in America* and *Vonnegut in Fact*, are essential resources.

When I was asked by Dan Simon of Seven Stories Press to collect and write commentaries on stories for *Complete Stories* by Kurt Vonnegut, I said I would do it only if I could have Klinkowitz as coeditor. I knew that he was the primary authority on Vonnegut's work. It was a wise choice, to put it mildly. An extra dividend was working with Jerry and his wife, Julie, in Cedar Falls, Iowa, and staying at the legendary Black Hawk Hotel, across the street from Joe's Coffee, which features the best fresh fruit muffins in America.

Ginger Strand's *The Brothers Vonnegut: Science and Fiction in the House of Magic* is I think the best biographical work on Kurt thus far, both artful and accurate. Strand is another generous colleague.

Christina Jarvis, a professor at the State University of New York at Fredonia, is the rising star of Vonnegut studies, and her lectures at the Kurt Vonnegut Museum and Library in Indianapolis have provided the greatest pleasure and enlightenment of the museum's Teaching Vonnegut course.

Max Goller, who created the Teaching Vonnegut course, gives generous and continuous support to my work. Teaching Vonnegut is offered every summer at the Vonnegut Museum in Indianapolis.

Thanks to Julia Whitehead and the Kurt Vonnegut Museum and Library for keeping Kurt's work alive and well in his hometown and reaching out to the world with classes, events, and festivities that celebrate his work and demonstrate its relevance.

Thanks to Kurt's lifelong friend Majie Failey, who saved letters, photographs, and memories for her delightful book *We Never Danced Cheek to Cheek: The Young Kurt Vonnegut in Indianapolis and Beyond*.

Charles J. Shields, author of a controversial biography of Vonnegut that did not find favor with Kurt's family and friends (including me), was nevertheless generous in sharing research, including important interviews with grandsons of Ida Young.

Phillip Hoose, a winner of the National Book Award for Young People's Literature, whose latest book, *Attucks!: Oscar Robertson and the Basketball Team Awakened a City*, is the best and most honest account of the great Oscar Robertson championship team, gave me the best advice for beginning a young adult book: "Go back to your high school, and talk to the students."

Daniel Comiskey commissioned me to write the essay "How an Old White Guy Got Woke" for *Indianapolis Monthly*. Pat LaMarche, activist, writer, head of the Charles Bruce Foundation, and supporter of films documenting friends of Kurt Vonnegut, commissioned the documentary producer Don Sawyer to begin filming the story of my racial education, from the Emmett Till murder trial and friendship with James Baldwin to my taking the workshop sponsored by Child Advocates in Indianapolis called Undoing Racism, now presented as Interrupting Racism. I have come to know black and white leaders who have become my friends as well as my educators. LaMarche is a great supporter of Vonnegut projects and is supporting film interviews of Kurt's friends.

Thanks as always to Dr. Jane Cohen of the Physicians Group of South Florida, who saved my life in Miami and continues to keep me extant.

* * *

I have been fortunate to find myself surrounded by the kindest and most supportive people in Indianapolis. No one has been a greater friend and supporter, both personal and professional, than the most brilliant of Indiana writers, Susan Neville, whose work is nationally recognized and honored. Her stunning book of short stories *The Town of Whispering Dolls* won the Catherine Doctorow Prize for "the best book of innovative fiction of 2019." Her first book of essays, *Indiana Winter*, evokes the essence of this place with the power of prayer. She is my guide, teacher, and benefactor, without whose help and support I might have given up the effort to "go home again" and fled back to Miami. I wish I could write a tribute to every valued friend here, but each knows their special role in my Hoosier salvation.

My life and work has progressed with the friendship of

the following people, listed here not in order of appreciation but as they pop into mind, starting with John Myers, whose untimely death last years was a blow to many; he was the most unselfish friend I ever had. I am fortunate to still have the following treasured friends: Patty McVeigh, Ken Bennet, Pam Frazier, Cindy Booth, Larry and Miriam Messing, Anne Belcher, Mary Morris, Glenda Soriano, Will Higgins, Jake Query, Donna and Gerry Foster, Georgia Cravey, Jim Lingenfelter, Tasha Jones, Pat Chastain, Kara Kavensky, Michael Gawdzok, Phyllis Boyd, Barb Shoup, Aleta Hodge, Nora Spitznagle, Cathy Gibson, Karen Kovacik, Crystal Rhodes, Jordan Schwartz, the Settles (Jim, Dolly, and Leslie), Violet Walker, everyone at the Red Key Tavern (a landmark, a legend, a haven), Dr. Stephen Beck and his fabulous staff, Ellen Crabb, Don Sawyer, Tim Hashko, Ian Woollen, and out of the blue, an unexpected blessing of the spirit, Mary Jane Mitchell.

Bless 'em all, bless 'em all,
the long and the short and the tall.
—"Bless 'Em All," ancient anthem of World War II

PHOTO CREDITS

reserved.

INDEX